A CANOEIST'S
SKETCHBOOK

$\mathcal{A}$ $\mathcal{C}$ANOEIST'S
$\mathcal{S}$KETCHBOOK

ROBERT KIMBER

Illustrations by
JERRY STELMOK

CHELSEA GREEN PUBLISHING COMPANY
POST MILLS, VERMONT

Chelsea Green Publishing Company
PO Box 130, Route 113
Post Mills, VT 05058-0130

Printed in the United States of America
First printing, July 1991

Library of Congress Cataloging-in-Publication Data
Kimber, Robert
        A canoeist's sketchbook / by Robert Kimber
        p.   cm.
        Includes bibliographical references.
        ISBN 0-930031-45-8 : $12.95.
        1. Canoes and canoeing.   2. Canoes and canoeing—
Maritime Provinces.   3. Canoes and canoeing—Quebec
(Province)   4. Canoes and canoeing—Maine.   I. Title.
GV783.K47   1991
797.1'22—dc20   91-18227
                                                    CIP

for John Miller

CONTENTS

PREFACE

This book is a collection of literary sketches about canoeing —some longer, some shorter, some practical, some reflective, some antic, some serious—but all in some way revealing, I hope, of what it is about canoeing, and wilderness canoeing in particular, that is so endlessly engaging, exciting, moving, satisfying, funny, and fulfilling. My original intention was not to limit these sketches to wilderness canoeing, but when I was all done with them, I found I hadn't written about much else. Unconscious as that principle of selection may have been, it is a true reflection of my allegiances and priorities. Canoe races and high-powered whitewater paddling are all well and good. But for me, what canoeing is really all about is getting out into big, wild country with a fly rod and some good friends along for company.

The origins of this book go back about five years when Ian Baldwin of Chelsea Green and I first discussed the possibility of my doing a canoe book. I said I'd be happy to oblige as long as he wanted neither a how-to book, which I feel is a genre that is already amply and admirably represented on the market, nor an account of an epic journey. I have been on quite a few canoe trips, but none that has crossed a continent or two and none that has marked the first descent of a hitherto unexplored 1,200-mile river in Outer Mongolia.

I wanted neither to instruct nor to chronicle. If I was going to write a book about canoeing, I realized, I wanted to do it for the same reason that prompts me to climb into a canoe in the first place, namely, to have some fun. I wanted to explore and poke around. I wanted to experience—or, in this case, to try to capture in words—the pleasures of leaning into the paddle all day, of picking my way down a shallow rapid on the pole, of setting up a comfortable camp, frying a fish and baking some biscuit. I wanted to see mile after mile of river and lake opening before me; to get an inkling from the wilderness we still have of what all creation was once like; to muse alone on a rock ledge at moonrise; to enjoy the company of old friends and new whose capacities for goofiness and hilarity become as boundless on a canoe journey as the big Canadian sky.

The sketch seemed the perfect medium for doing what I wanted to do. It catches experience on the wing, and many of the pieces here began as jottings in my river notebooks. The sketch does not attempt to give the whole picture but tries instead to capture the essence of a moment, a scene, a personality, a process, or a place, highlighting only those details that have particularly caught the writer's eye. It tends, too, to be a companionable medium, chatty, conversational, digressive. It is playful and whimsical at heart. Like a beagle on scent, it will go wherever its nose takes it, yelping happily and tail awag. And because the beagle is my totem animal, I've followed my own nose in choosing what I would write about and how I would write about it.

The pieces that deal with gear and technique here, while they may convey some information the reader will find useful, are as playful and philosophical in intent as they are practical; for in canoeing, as in fishing or sailing, what we use and how we use it is not only a matter of efficiency and efficacy but also one of style, an expression of how we see the world and ourselves in it. And then, because gear and technique are integral parts of an enterprise that is such great fun, they are fun in themselves, fun to think about and talk about, fun to tinker with and constantly improve upon.

One can't help being opinionated in these matters, but I hope my opinions fall short of arrogance.

The reason for the alphabetical sequence of these pieces is just plain potluck. I didn't know how else to order them, and as it turned out fate and the alphabet were kind to me. They yielded a mix of the long and the short, of anecdote, rumination, and practicality, that went down smoothly. They put "Backwards" at the front, and they let "Wilderness" have the last word. I couldn't have done better if I'd worked at it. So I didn't.

Two other editorial points are perhaps worth mentioning: masculine and feminine personal pronouns are used interchangeably throughout the book where the antecedent is a canoeist, paddler, poler, or whoever of unspecified sex. This usage reflects the reality of my experience, which has been that wilderness canoeing, like life, is not the exclusive province of males and that many of the ablest paddlers and most boon of boon companions on the river are women.

The brief "Notes on Readings and Gear" at the end of the book don't even begin to list all the literature or the sources of equipment a paddler might find useful. All the notes do is provide enough information on the few publications and items mentioned in the text to enable a reader to chase any of them down. Or, in the case of homemade items, like canoe poles and paddles, to find instructions for making them.

Lastly, of course, I have to say that whatever else this book may be it is a declaration of love to the bend in the river and the expanse of the big lake, to black spruce and dwarf birch. And it is a missive of affection, respect, and gratitude, too, to all my fellow travelers, both those who appear in these pages and those who don't. First on that list is my lifetime friend, John Miller. Then come three who have already crossed the big river: George Dennison, my neighbor in Temple, with whom I took several memorable trips; my father, Frank Kimber, who put me in a canoe at a very early age; and Don Yeaton, at whose heels I trotted over much of western Maine and who showed me that while it might be uncomfortable to fall out of a canoe on the Dead River in late November, it was not necessarily fatal.

In recent years, I've had the good fortune to paddle with three canoeing luminaries: Alexandra and Garrett Conover, owners and operators of North Woods Ways, Maine's most distinctive guiding service, and Jerry Stelmok, who builds some of the world's finest wood-and-canvas canoes and who was kind enough to grace these pages with his drawings. Though all three are my juniors in age, they are much my seniors in canoe savvy and woods wisdom. (You know you've hit middle age when you look around you on the river and the people in the other boats are all younger, tougher, and smarter than you are.) I've learned so much from them, both consciously and by osmosis, that it would be impossible to acknowledge fully my debt to them, and it would be more than impossible to thank them adequately for the pleasure of their extraordinary company and the gift of their friendship.

But, undaunted, I'll try anyhow: Thank you, Jerry. Thank you, Garrett. Thank you, Alexandra.

Robert Kimber
Temple, Maine
April 1991

$\mathcal{B}$ACKWARDS

No MATTER HOW you look at it, the traditional North American canoe is symmetrical. If you look down on it from above or up at it from below, it is widest in the middle and tapers identically toward both ends. If you look at it from the side, the sheer lines are the same at both ends. In a traditional canoe, there is no bow and no stern. Or rather there are two bows. If you put seats in the boat, then you commit yourself, and you can say, "Aha, this is the front, and this is the back." You may think you know now which is bow and which is stern, but the canoe will ignore those definitions. It will respond pretty much the same way whether you are pushing or pulling it forward or backward with paddle, pole, or line.

For that, the wilderness paddler can be grateful because going backwards is often far more important than going forwards, and in the course of many maneuvers, bow and stern may well trade places. A poler may start snubbing her way down one route, decide she doesn't like it, and back up a few yards to pick another route. Or someone lining down a rapid may decide to pull his boat back upstream to set it out a little farther into the current. If direction of travel determines what is bow and what is stern, then in both these

1

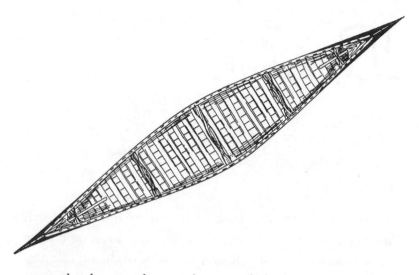

examples bow and stern have traded places. Because the canoe has a "bow" at both ends that trade can take place easily and instantaneously. These same simple maneuvers would be next to impossible for a square-sterned boat with its stern upstream. A square-sterned boat can be lined with its stern downstream, but the thought of poling a square-ender down an intricate rapid gives me the willies. It would be a bit like trying to run a slalom course on a toboggan instead of skis.

The beautiful, brilliant, symmetrical, traditional canoe does away with all such willies. Because it is streamlined and identical at both ends, it permits precise and predictable control going forwards or backwards and eases not just poling and lining but also the backpaddling techniques needed for safe river travel—backpaddling to travel slower than the current, backpaddling to prevent shipping big waves, back ferrying to cross currents.

There is no place where the canoe's ability to run backwards and forwards, upstream or down, and to pivot around its own centerpoint is more dramatically evident than in the hands of a good slalom racer. At reverse gates, slalom paddlers have to drop their boats through the gates backwards, looking over their shoulders to see where they're going.

All these backward maneuvers are, of course, intentional, but there is also the unintentional backward maneuver, the maneuver in which your bow becomes your stern without your say-so, the maneuver in which some exquisitely camouflaged rock or some vagary of the current you had not reckoned with spins you around and sends you zipping downstream—not through one little slalom gate but through a maze of rocks intent on having you for lunch.

In such a situation, rejoice that you are in a canoe. Remember, your boat is still traveling with one of its bows first; it is just you, not the canoe, who happens to be looking the wrong way. Relax, take stock over your shoulder, look nonchalant. The river may give you a break and let you turn yourself right way around in a convenient eddy on the way down. Or you may have to finish out the drop backwards. Either way, if you're still afloat when you reach the bottom, you can try to convince your buddies that you meant to run it that way.

Or if they haven't been watching, you can just turn yourself around and pretend you ran the drop frontwards. What other boat but the traditional, symmetrical, open canoe would ever permit of such an innocent, face-saving lie?

*B*AGS, BOXES, BASKETS, BACKPACKS, AND THE PURSUIT OF ELEGANCE

ONCE YOU'VE ASSEMBLED all the stuff you need for a canoe journey, you then have to pack it into something to get it from your living room floor to the car, from the car to the canoe, from canoe to campsite, from campsite to canoe, from one end of the portage trail to the other. What should you use? Suitcases? Froot Loops cartons recycled from the corner grocery?

If you consult the experts, you will not find universal agreement. In *The Complete Wilderness Paddler* Davidson and Rugge champion the packframe, praising the padded shoulder straps, the contoured frame, and the hip belt, which all ease the carrying of heavy loads. They grant, however, that packframes are gawky things to fit into a canoe. Cliff Jacobson, in his equally authoritative *Canoeing Wild Rivers*, votes for the Duluth pack, praising its capaciousness, its efficient use of space in the canoe, its lack of breakable parts, and the ease of waterproofing it. He grants, however, that it is "unsophisticated and uncomfortable to carry."

Faced with this divergence of opinion among giants, what is one to do? In the best tradition of the wishy-washy politician who does not want to offend either constituency, I will declare them both right and then go on to say that I and most of the folks I travel with use Duluth packs only rarely and packframes never. But let me stress once more, my fellow North Americans, that in our great pluralistic societies there are many ways to pack for a canoe trip, and the only right way is the way that works for you.

Like just about everything else in canoeing, preferences for certain kinds of packs and for packing strategies are part of a personal style that each of us develops for him or her-self and that is influenced by any number of factors. What part of the country do you come from? From whom did you learn canoeing, and what packs did your teachers use? What kind of country do you usually travel? What are your personal quirks? And for any given trip, there are trip-specific questions. How long will you be out? How many are in your party? Do the rivers and terrain you'll be traveling demand the lightest, most Spartan of outfits or can you afford a somewhat heavier, cushier one?

The Duluth pack is the traditional canoe pack in the Midwest. Midwestern paddlers grow up with it, learning to appreciate its many virtues and live with its few drawbacks. The woven ash packbasket is still a common sight on Maine rivers, even though Davidson and Rugge would happily consign both it and the Duluth pack to museums exhibiting quaint canoeing gear of yore. On the trip they chronicle in *The Complete Wilderness Paddler*—the Moisie River in Quebec—their packframes make a lot of sense because that trip seems to call for a lot of portaging around and in and out of deep canyons. Under those conditions, ease in carrying is a top priority, and luxuries that add weight and bulk to your outfit are probably best left at home.

But if you will not be doing three mountain-goat portages a day, there's much to be said for the packbasket; and even if you are doing a lot of tough portaging and you happen to like packbaskets, as I do, you may want to put in a good word for them anyway. Just about everyone recognizes their value for carrying hard, gawky items like cooking gear and thermos bottles, which, if carried in soft packs, tend to abrade cloth and poke holes in your back. But I'm partial to packbaskets as food packs, too. Lined or double-lined with rubberized army-surplus laundry bags, and with everything inside that could be damaged by water packed in Ziploc or freezer bags, they keep your stores doubly or triply water-proofed, and they float. The skids on the bottom keep them up out of the bilge water in the boat and up out of the muck in a rainy camp. Also, it is much easier to root around in a firm-sided container than in a flippy, floppy, soft pack.

Theoretically, of course, one should never have to root. One is supposed to be so well organized that last night's cocoa never winds up buried beneath tomorrow morning's pancake mix or vice versa. But realistically, the day inevita- bly comes when I have to dig and paw and scrabble for that stray stick of soya margarine that has obeyed the first law of pack dynamics, which states that whatever it is you want will be at the very bottom of the last pack you search through. In short, if you've got to root, a packbasket makes for the happiest rooting.

On the portage trail, the packbasket's narrow shape and rounded contours keep it from hanging up in the alders, and it provides a platform on which you can neatly carry some soft duffel.

So what's wrong with it? Well, the webbing used for the harness and shoulder straps on most packbaskets is narrow and not hugely comfortable. Adding wider shoulder straps is an option, though that's not an alteration I've ever felt strongly enough about to actually make. Two medium-sized baskets standing back to back fit into any traveling canoe neatly enough, but they do stick up in the air a bit, and if you want to lash your load down, they're an awkward item to tie into a canoe in a very shipshape way, unless you lay them down on their backs or bellies.

Another venerable item among the stiff-sided gear carriers is the wanigan. Shortened from *atawangan*, which appears in some form in all the Algonquian languages and means, roughly, "a container for stores," the word gained currency throughout the northeastern United States and the Canadian Maritimes in a number of variants: wangan, wan- gun, wannigan, wammikin. In logging parlance, it could mean either the boat that carried the cook's outfit and stores on river drives or a chest used for those same purposes. Today, it means only a box canoeists use mostly for transporting cook kits, though some paddlers may carry food in it as well. The traditional wanigan is made of light wood and measures roughly twenty-eight inches long by twelve wide by fifteen deep. Quarter-inch marine plywood serves nicely for the sides and lid, one-inch pine for the bottom and ends; and the dimensions can of course be altered to suit what you want to carry. The point is simply to have a box that fits crosswise in the boat just about anywhere amidships and is narrow enough to leave plenty of room for other packs.

Wanigans are particulary convenient for large parties of, say, six to ten because they easily accomodate large pots and pans and keep all the kitchen gear stashed in a neat and easily accessible package. The top of a wanigan makes a great cutting board and breadboard for the cook and a mini-buffet table when the meal is ready to serve. If you keep only cooking gear in wanigans, they are light enough to be shouldered for short portages. For longer ones, they can be carried with a tumpline with soft duffel stacked on top of them. If you put heavy foodstuffs in them too, then they become cumbersome to portage. A light box is easy to handle; a heavy one is not.

A wanigan used only to carry kitchen utensils doesn't have to be waterproof, and so the simple wooden box is quite adequate to the task. If you want a watertight wanigan, the market will oblige. When made of plastic or aluminum and equipped with watertight seals, wanigans seem to be called "dry boxes." They're fairly expensive, and the dimensions of some of the larger ones make them ungainly in a canoe and impossible to portage without the aid of a mule team. They are designed primarily for no-portage raft trips, not crawl-around-in-the-brush-and-swamp canoe trips. I cannot imagine what would ever induce me to buy one.

However widely expert opinions on the ideal pack may diverge, there's one point on which everyone agrees: No matter what packs you use, your waterproofing system has to be flawless. For foodstuffs like flour and rice, for your clothes and your sleeping bag—that holy of holies, that ultimate haven of comfort and delight—you need absolutely bomb-proof protection.

This is where the pursuit of elegance comes in. An elegant outfit is one that keeps everything dry that needs to be kept dry yet requires a minimum of fuss to operate. The simple, wooden wanigan is elegant. You unhitch the one strap that holds the lid on, lift the lid, and there you have your whole kitchen kit ready at hand. The ideal pack for food, sleeping bags, and clothes would operate just as simply but also be waterproof and durable enough to last for several seasons of fairly rigorous use.

Plastic bags in a variety of forms are the key ingredient in most waterproofing systems, and though plastic can be a great boon to canoeists, it can also be the enemy of elegance. The obvious and cheap expedient would seem to be plastic garbage bags, but there isn't anything worse. They're so thin that they develop pinholes and tear in no time, so you need two or three layers of them, and even then they afford unreliable protection that won't stand up to much more than a week's hard use. Not to mention that you will have to open and close three plastic bags every time you want to get at what's inside. Call it one of my personal quirks, but by the time I've untwisted the tops of three rattly, crinkly plastic garbage bags to take something out of a pack, then retwisted those same tops, securing each one with heavy elastic, I'm just about ready to quit canoeing and take up golf. Then if you consider, on top of the nuisance factor, the number of tattered plastic bags you add to the world's growing junk pile, there is no case left for garbage bags at all.

For food in packbaskets, the aforementioned Ziploc bags, freezer bags, and rubberized laundry bags provide excellent waterproofing plus relative ease of access. For clothes and sleeping bags, the most elegant solution is the PVC-coated Dacron bag pioneered some twelve years ago by Northwest River Supplies. The roll-down closures on these bags make them easy to open and close, and if the bag is stuffed full enough so that the four closure straps can be snugged down firmly—yet not so full that the top can't be folded over several times—these bags are waterproof under all but the most dire conditions. (The most dire conditions are a boat pinned in a heavy current where the pressure on the bag closure could be immense.) If you anticipate the possibility of such conditions, you can take waterproofing a step further. Stuff your sleeping bag into a nylon stuff sack; put bag and stuff sack inside a 4-mil plastic bag, squeeze the air out of the plastic bag, twist the top, fold the twist, and seal it with a heavy rubber band cut from an old inner tube; finally, put the whole thing into a second stuff sack slightly larger than the first. The inner and outer stuff sacks protect the plastic bag from abrasion from both within and without. Use the same system for a set of emergency clothes.

I put the emergency clothes at the very bottom of my Northwest River bag, stuff all my other clothing in loose, and put the sleeping bag in last. This system gives me easy access to the sleeping bag and changes of clothes yet assures me a dry set of clothes and a dry bed if the bag ever should leak.

Cliff Jacobson has sagely observed, "Waterproof bags tend to be either dependable and awkward to use, or undependable and easy to use." Everyone has to figure out his or her own dependability, convenience, and durability equation and act accordingly. For soft duffel, the Northwest River bag suits my needs in all departments. I don't toss my gear up onto river banks bristling with sharp, flinty rocks. In fact I don't toss my gear anywhere, anytime, so a Northwest River bag can last me many seasons and spare me messing around with heavy-duty (6-mil) plastic Duluth pack liners, which, though vastly superior to 2-mil garbage bags, I still find irksome to roll and unroll all the time. The ease of using the Northwest River bag does great things for my sanity, and being a conservative soul, I avoid situations where I might put the bag to the ultimate test. I know that a properly packed and closed Northwest River bag tied into a canoe can bounce down a couple of miles of rapids without leaking. That seems to me a fair compromise between elegance and waterproofness.

So here I am, in defiance of my betters, confessing that I like packbaskets, wanigans, and Northwest River bags. What can I say? For the kinds of waters I travel and for the kind of person I am, they work. Which is not to say I'll never do things differently. I used to think that someday I would develop the absolutely perfect canoe kit and packing system, that I would someday be truly finished with my outfit, that I'd know exactly what to take every time, that I'd own the perfect packs, the perfect spoons, the perfect condiment bag, that I'd attain to perfect efficiency and elegance. Yes, elegance. I would never make a wasted motion, never have one gratuitous plastic bag or one pair of socks along that went unused on the trip. I'd have everything down to such a perfect science that, except for devising menus, I'd never have to think about what to take or how to take it again.

Toward that blessed end, I've kept meticulous lists of everything I take on trips—clothes, gear, food quantities—and made notes on what I used, what I didn't use, what worked and didn't work, what worked but could have worked better. The basic system is in place, readily adaptable to a three-day trip in Maine in July or a three-week one in Labrador in September. But I know now that I'll never reach the state of unthinking, ultimate perfection because the refining process never ends. I'm always discovering, or learning from a fellow traveler, how to make camp just a little more comfortable, how to cook a little better meal, how to do everything from brushing my teeth to setting up a rain tarp just a little more efficiently. Ultimate elegance can be pursued, it seems, but never achieved.

$\mathcal{B}$IG FISH

IF YOU'RE WONDERING whether I'm going to tell a big-fish story, let me put your mind at rest. The answer is yes. But this story is not about *a* big fish. It's about *the* big fish. That's an important distinction.

In the yarns of fisherfolk, big fish swarm as thick as smelts in springtime, probably because bigness is a relative term. The other day when I was out thrashing around in back of my place with a brush scythe, I heard some kids' voices coming through the wall of alders between the house and the little trout stream that runs through our land. So I wandered down to the water to see how they were doing. There were two boys about ten and twelve.

"How you making out?" I asked.

The older boy didn't say anything. He just reached into his creel after casting a glance at me that I took to mean, "Mister, once you've seen what I've got to show, you'll understand why words are superfluous."

He hauled out for my inspection a nice, chunky brook trout about a foot long, long enough, at any rate, that it couldn't lie flat in his creel; and its head and tail were already curling up from being in those cramped quarters.

Now for little Temple Stream, that's a big fish.

"Wow!" I said, duly appreciative. "Where'd you get him?"

"In that pool just above Mitchells' footbridge," the kid said. "And you should have seen the *other* one. It was *twice* as big, but I couldn't get him to strike for anything. I must have tickled his nose with my worm for ten minutes, but he wouldn't budge."

Twice as big? Well, maybe. Even if it was only half again as big, or a third or a quarter, it was still a big fish for our backyard stream and not half bad for any waters. But regardless of how big either of these fish was—the one the kids had caught and the one they hadn't—we all understood that both of them were merely big fish. Just about any outing, except one on which you've been skunked or have caught only such minute fish that you're ashamed to mention them, provides stuff for a big-fish report. If you've caught any respectable fish at all and one of them happens to be larger than the others, that fish is the big fish of the day and worthy of comment as such. Better still is the even larger fish, like the trout the kids did not hook, that you encountered but did not land. Maybe you just saw it; maybe it rose to your fly and you missed the strike; maybe you actually had it on for a few minutes, but then it threw the hook.

These are the big fish that make up the daily bread of fishing. They can be of any species, and they can be taken on any kind of tackle. I'm grateful for them all—the twenty-five-inch pickerel on a Rapala minnow, the two-and-a-half-pound smallmouth on a bass bug, the four-pound lake trout taken on a trolled streamer right after ice-out.

But the big fish is different from all of these. The big fish is a lifelong quest. The big fish is every fisherman's or fisherwoman's piscine Holy Grail. For Hemingway's old fisher-

man it was that huge marlin the sharks chewed to smither-
eens. For a kid on the lower Mississippi it's a monster river
cat. Your big fish can be only one kind of fish. There may
be fish that grow much larger and fish that are considered
far nobler. The opinion of the world does not matter. Your
big fish has chosen you as much as you have chosen it. It is
woven into the tapestry of your personal history. It is your
fishly destiny.

Your big fish is like your mate. You know there are others that are more brilliant and more beautiful, measured by
some objective, abstract standards that mean nothing to
you; but yours has a special aura, a special glow. I've been
told by several fly-fishing fanatics that my big fish should be
an Atlantic salmon or at least a landlocked salmon, one of
those silvery, leaping, pirouetting creatures. Well, by rights,
maybe it should. I've caught landlocked salmon, and I
know that every word spoken in praise of them is true. But
my big fish is still a brook trout—hook-jawed, deep in the
body, red-bellied, square-tailed, dotted with those evanescent

rainbow spots. And it has to be encountered with a fly rod.

My big fish inhabits the submarine world of my soul and will not be replaced by any other. It is an obsession, the Moby Fish of my modest, un-Melville-sized imagination, an underwater beast that swims through my dreams, leaves me marveling, slathering, drooling, aching, yearning. It is just as likely she as he. There is surely something deeply erotic about it, the essence of our fleshly life as well as of our transcendental longings, the incarnation of *amor mundi*.

The pursuit of the big fish may be a quest, but you can't make a project of it. You can't make up your mind and say, "Now, by gum, it's high time I caught my big fish, and I'm going to go out and do it." At the same time, you can't stay home, fishing in Temple Stream, and expect to meet the big fish either. You'll need your canoe to get there, paddling, lining, portaging. You have to go more than halfway, saying each time you go, "I'm ready but I expect nothing." Or better yet, saying nothing at all. And you won't know you are there until you are there.

The river is wide, not huge but wide, perhaps a hundred yards here where it rushes through a labyrinth of boulders before dropping over a couple of ledges that are runnable if you hit them just right. The water surges by with the authority of a huge Labrador watershed behind it. Rivers in this territory do not dry up in August. They may run deeper in the spring, but they always run deep.

My fishing partner John Miller and I have poled upstream from our campsite on a grassy point, tied the canoe up, and are working our way along the bank, fishing from the ledgy fingers that project out into the water, hopping from ledge to rock to another rock so we can reach just a little more water. The fishing is so good that it would be ungrateful, ungracious, almost downright obscene to wish it any better. We're catching pound-and-a-half, two-and-a-half-pound trout often enough to keep the appetite keenly whetted but not so often that we take anything for granted.

I've worked a fair section of the river, reaching as much water as I can from the bank, and now I'm tantalized by what lies beyond the range of my cast. I go back to the canoe, find a rock that will make a decent anchor, tie a rope around it. John is a quarter mile or more upstream, so I head out into the current alone, drop my anchor, start working the midstream eddies and the pockets behind the rocks.

Nothing.

I drop downstream a few yards. Still nothing. Again I move, and still again. The water is delicious. There have to be huge trout lurking everywhere I cast, but no action. I'm fishing a fluffy yellow and red invention called Sarah's Charms on a 5X tippet, a combo that has worked wonders so far this morning. But has some change come over the fish and the river in the last fifteen minutes? Is what used to be right now wrong? Or have the fish just decided it's time to pack it in this morning?

And then, of course, when I am least expecting to, I meet the Big Fish. It strikes with an authority that makes the word "strike" seem cheap and tinny. What I feel, telegraphed to me up that line and rod and into my hand and arm and heart, is like the cello picking up the theme of the slow movement in Haydn's "Emperor" Quartet, a melody utterly familiar, but sounding now with a richness and fullness that would bring tears to my eyes if I were not now suddenly faced with the need to play the biggest trout of my life on a 5X tippet and so have no time for idle tears.

I saw the beast roll as it took off with the fly, a great flash

17

of red, a huge, sleek, animate torpedo heading downstream on my spiderweb of a leader. It looked as long and deep as the blade of my canoe paddle. That's thirty by seven inches. All right, I know the record weight for a brookie is fourteen and a half pounds, the length, thirty-one and a half inches. Notice I said my fish looked as long and deep as the blade of my canoe paddle. Maybe it wasn't that long. Maybe it was only—only!—two feet long. I don't know how long it was. But I know it was humongous. My aging edition of *McClane's Standard Fishing Encyclopedia* says, in prose I can only call encyclopedic, "Fish of over 5 pounds may be considered exceptional."

My fish was over five pounds, way over; and I'm glad I may consider it exceptional. It bolted with the current, tearing line off the reel, then bored back in toward the canoe. Control was out of the question. All I could hope to do was keep the fragile link between it and me intact, just stay in touch. At that moment, the idea of catching this fish was the furthest thing from my mind. Sooner capture the river itself, all that fluid speed and power. But before too many seconds had passed, a faint hope stirred in me after all. Maybe I would be able to lead this creature of a lifetime to the side of my canoe, to encounter it face to face, to pay it my deepest respects, to look briefly into an eye that saw every day what I could never see, and then to gently roll the barbless hook free of its jaw.

That was my fondest wish. What was most likely to foil it was the stupid anchor rope. One wrap around that, and my 5X leader was history. So when the fish drove toward the boat, I put as much pressure on him as I dared. I coaxed him back out into open water, I teased and cajoled, I pleaded and prayed and begged; and at some point in this struggle I really began to think, "Yes, I will bring this fish to hand. It is not impossible."

But then a breeze came rushing downstream, and the rock that had been able to keep my canoe stationary in the current was not able to withstand the pressure of both wind and water. The next minute was pure Harpo Marx on the river, the most sublime moment of my angling life blending inexorably into the most ridiculous.

Slowly, oh so slowly, the canoe broke loose and started drifting downstream. I could hear the anchor clicking against the rock bottom as the boat picked up momentum. Now it was moving right along, and the fish was heading back upstream again. I could see the anchor line pulled out taut to the port side of the canoe, and I could see the line knifing toward it. Even if the fish stopped, the anchor rope would soon drift across the line.

I couldn't put the rod down, pull the anchor, and paddle into shore. I considered jumping out of the boat and trying to flounder to shore, but the water was too deep. Even if I didn't break the leader or the rod when I jumped, how could I swim and play a fish at the same time? And even if I managed that somehow, I didn't have enough time to get the fish clear of the boat and that dangling rope. Maybe if I grabbed a paddle with one hand and tried to swing the canoe around and away from the rope while I kept some pressure on the rod with the other hand?

There just weren't any good ideas, and as I grabbed the paddle to try to execute my last bad one, rope and leader crossed, there was another flash of color, and I knew it was all over with my fishly destiny.

I ranted, I screamed, I yelled at the bright but unfeeling heavens.

"Oh, *no!* I can't goddam *believe* it!"

I pulled in the anchor rope, went ashore, and stared at the leader wrapped around that rope. Pathetic, that little wisp of nylon.

From upstream, John had seen the arch in my rod, seen the canoe start to slide down the river, seen my absurd dance with paddle in one hand and rod in the other, seen me raise my fist to the sky and rail at the gods. He came back down to meet me.

"I've just lost the biggest frigging fish I'll ever hope to see in my life," I told him.

"How big?" he asked as we climb into the canoe.

"See this paddle blade?" I said. "That big. Or close anyway."

"Wow!" John said.

I felt like a high-school sophomore whose first love had just dumped him. I knew I'd never get over it. I was destroyed for life. The thought of my fish in someone else's arms was more than I could bear. What if some lout with a spinning rod came along next week and caught that fish on a Dardevle? Oh, God, what unspeakable anguish! What barbarity! Just thinking about it sent me into frenzies of jealous rage.

Well, some time has passed. The wounds are scarred over, and I guess I can honestly say with Tennyson, 'tis better to have hooked and lost than never to have hooked at all. When I'm feeling particularly mellow and philosophical I can even believe that in the great cosmic order of things my true fishly destiny was not to catch that fish. Ahab didn't catch Moby Dick either. The great white whale is still out there, and so is that trout big as a paddle blade. And when I really think about it, I even know that fish will never fall

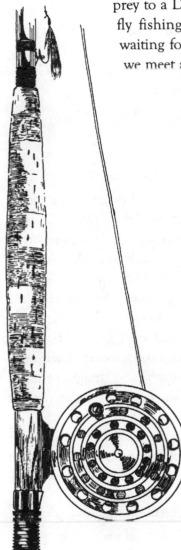

prey to a Dardevle. My Big Fish believes in
fly fishing only. He's still out there, not
waiting for me, not holding his breath till
we meet again, but just out there.

*B*OUYANCY

BECAUSE CANOEISTS LIKE to stay afloat, buoyancy is a matter of no little interest to them, an interest that usually finds its first expression in their choice of boats. The wilderness traveler will look for a boat that has not only enough volume to float him, a partner, and all their stuff but also a design that turns away waves that are eager to climb aboard. The solo whitewater canoes that expert open-boat paddlers are now taking into waters previously plied only by decked boats have those same features but carried to extremes. Their exaggeratedly blunt stems, cheeky quarters, and straight or flared sides give them added buoyancy for riding up on waves that skinnier boats would dive into.

And then the prudent whitewater boater venturing into big stuff will equip his boat with flotation bags to insure that it is every bit as buoyant upside down as it is rightside up, just in case he should dump. The additional flotation will see to it that the canoe minus paddler continues to ride high and does not fill up with water, hang up on a rock, and either get torn to pieces or pinned beyond rescue in some inaccessible corner.

To insure her own personal buoyancy if she should become detached from her boat, any and every canoeist should wear a life jacket. It's interesting to note that paddlers, authoritative books about canoeing, and the catalogs of emporia that cater to the serious canoeing trade all continue to call life jackets "life jackets, life vests," or "life preservers." The U.S. Coast Guard, the organization charged by federal law with rating, inspecting, testing, and certifying life jackets, insists on calling them "personal flotation devices." Well, all right. I suppose if I were the commandant of the U.S. Coast Guard I might want a generic term, too. Granted, not all the devices that provide persons with flotation are jackets or vests, nor do any of them guarantee that they can preserve life. A boater pinned underwater or churned around indefinitely in the reversing current of a sousehole will drown whether dutifully clad in a life jacket or not, and a life jacket offers some, but not enough, protection against hypothermia in a cold-water upset.

So I suppose one could argue that the bureaucratic pedantry of the Coast Guard is not mere pedantry after all but another small victory in the human struggle to say what we mean. Technically correct as the phrase may be, however, it is not exactly catchy, and I never expect to see the day when a paddler about to step into her boat says to her partner, "Hey, Charlie, hand me my personal flotation device."

The abbreviation "PFD" is a lesser burden for the tongue and has gained some ground in technical and quasi-technical writings that describe the features and weigh the respective merits of various PFDs. It does save some space, but I doubt it will ever win much favor in the spoken language either. Who wants to wear something whose initials could

23

just as well stand for "Peoria Fire Department" and that would sound like "pfudd" if you tried to pronounce it? No, "PFD" just doesn't lift the spirit.

A life jacket, by contrast, does. More importantly still, it lifts the body when the body is in dire need of lifting. Who, having ever felt the firm, sustaining hand of a life jacket hauling him from the roily depths to the surface, can ever doubt that a life jacket is indeed a life jacket, a far nobler garment than any mere dinner jacket or sports jacket or jean jacket? The Coast Guard may want to quibble and call a jacket that does not make you invulnerable a personal flotation device, but for those who know and love them, life jackets will continue to be life jackets.

The Coast Guard lists five categories of PFDs. Type I PFDs are the huge, puffy, beer-bellied orange monsters you'll find under the benches in ferry boats. They'll keep you floating face up even if you're unconscious, and so they probably come closer to the literal definition of "life preserver" better than any other type. But they're so huge and bulky that no paddler wearing one could lower his arms enough to reach the water with a paddle. Type II is the orange horse collar you can buy at discount stores and super drugstores for six or seven dollars. This type, too, will float you face up. If the flotation is provided by kapok stuffed into plastic liners, however, a hole poked in the plastic will let water into the kapok, soak it, and make the horsecollar function more like a millstone than a life preserver. Closed-cell foam substituted for kapok makes horsecollars more reliable, but it still does not make them any more comfortable. They chafe the neck mercilessly, and though the bulky tubes strapped to one's chest don't make paddling impossible, they are a damned nuisance.

Type III PFDs are the vest designs that close with a zipper down the front and use closed-cell foam for flotation. The foam may be in the form of large flat panels in a nylon shell or in long blocks sewn into tubelike compartments in the shell. These jackets do not float you face up, which is no doubt why the Coast Guard, honing its terminology a little more each year, is now requiring manufacturers to call them "flotation aids" rather than life jackets or life preservers. But paddlers are rarely unconscious when they take a swim, and the advantages of this design far outweigh the disadvantages. These jackets are not bulky; they leave the body and arms unhampered for paddling; they provide padding for the back and sides in rocky rapids; and they help keep you warm on cold days.

Type IVs are tossables, things like floating cushions and lifesaving rings, devices anybody can agree should be called devices, not jackets. Type V includes everything else: the buoyant belts waterskiers use, commercial whitewater rafting jackets, and so on.

When you look at the label in a life jacket, it will give you some numbers that never made much sense to me, and most articles and ads about life jackets toss them around cavalierly, assuming that every reader knows what they mean. For the benefit of the rest of you who have forgotten your high-school physics and have always nodded sagely but didn't really know from Shinola when somebody talked at you about buoyancy in life jackets, let me share the results of my research.

The label in any Type III jacket meant for adult use will contain this legend: "Buoyant material provides a minimum buoyant force of 15.5 pounds." The label will also tell you that this personal flotation device is approved for use by persons weighing more than 90 pounds. What is buoyant force anyway, and how can a lousy little 15.5 pounds of it hold up somebody who weighs 90 pounds, much less 190 or 235?

Archimedes, that old Greek mathematician who also figured out how to use levers, came up with the answer long before the invention of life jackets. One day when he was climbing into his bath, he noticed that the tub spilled over when he lowered his bulk into it. This started him thinking about things like specific gravity and water displacement, and he was so delighted with what he could deduce from his overflowing bath that he leapt out of the tub and ran home naked, shouting "Eureka!" all the way.

The puzzle Archimedes was working on that day was one that Hieron, king of Syracuse, had set for him. Hieron wanted to know if a crown made for him was really pure gold, as purported, or whether it had an admixture of silver in it. What Archimedes realized in the bathtub was that if he put the crown into a vessel of water and measured the overflow and then did the same thing with a piece of pure gold of the same weight, he'd have the answer to the king's question. If the crown had an alloy of silver in it, it would displace more water than the piece of gold would because silver weighs less per volume (i.e., has a lower specific gravity) than gold.

The principle Archimedes developed from all this is known, fairly enough, as Archimedes' principle or the principle of buoyancy, which says that a body immersed in a fluid is buoyed up by a force equal to the weight of the fluid it displaces. If you take a life jacket and toss it onto the water, it will float, hardly denting the surface because it has a very low specific gravity. That is, measured against the standard of water, one liter of which weighs 1,000 grams and has a specific gravity of 1.0, it has little weight per volume. To be more precise, my life jacket weighs 77 grams per liter and therefore has a specific gravity of 0.077. To find out its buoyant force when fully immersed, you have to yank it under the surface of the water in Archimedes' brimful bathtub. If you do, about 13 liters of water, weighing 13 kilograms (or 28.6 pounds) will slop over the sides. And if you look up the figures on an Extrasport Hi-Float jacket, which is designed to provide an extra margin of flotation and safety in big water, you'll find that its design bouyancy rating is 26.12 pounds (i.e., 28.6 minus the weight of the jacket itself).

If you sank 13 liters of lead in the tub, it too would spill 28 pounds worth of water, and the buoyant force at work on it would also be be 13 kilos or 28.6 pounds. But because the specific gravity of lead is 11.35, a buoyant force of 13 kilos is as nothing in this configuration. The 13 liters of lead weigh 147.55 kilos in the air. Subtract the buoyant force of 13 kilos, and they still weigh 134.55 kilos in water. The gravitational pull overwhelms the buoyant force, and the lead sinks even faster than a stone.

The human body's performance in water clearly falls between that of lead and that of the life jacket. Our specific gravity hovers a bit above or below 1.0 because much of our body tissue is made up of water and because the parts of us that are denser than water (muscle, bone) are offset by parts that are less dense (lungs, fat). When we jump into the water, we almost sink or barely float, depending on how you look at it. If we take a deep breath and hold it, we float; if we let the breath out, we sink. Body type also affects our floating ability. An obese person may float without benefit

27

of a deep breath, and a skinny one may go down despite a lungful of air. Doctors can calculate the amount of body fat we're hauling around by weighing us in both air and water and figuring our body density from that.

The applications of all this to life jackets are these: Our bodies displace their own weight in the water and are therefore buoyed up by a force equal to that weight; because—depending on a number of factors—our specific gravity can vary from slightly above to slightly below 1.0, we are sometimes weightless in water and can float without any assistance; and we sometimes weigh about ten to twelve pounds in water and so need assistance to stay afloat.

Tests conducted on twenty-two individuals many years ago by the Mellon Institute and reported in *American White-water* bore this out. They showed that during inspir-ation zero pounds of buoyant force were needed to keep the head above water. During expiration, twelve pounds were needed. Hence, the Coast Guard's minimum requirement of 15.5 pounds buoyant force in an adult life jacket provides enough flotation to do the job plus a little extra for good measure.

Why, then, the high-floating jackets with twenty or more pounds of buoyant force? Aren't they overkill? If you'll be paddling primarily on ponds and flatwater rivers, they are; and there are plenty of whitewater canoeists paddling—and sometimes swimming—quite heavy water with the standard 15.5 pounds of flotation. For paddlers who frequent Class IV and V water, however, the high floaters have become the rule. The extra boost they supply can help you come up for air that much sooner and more often if you take a swim in huge standing waves and foamy, aerated stuff. I'm no whitewater powerhouse, and Class III is about as wild and wooly as I usually go. But the swims I've taken even in that fairly modest class have made me grateful for the ten or twelve extra pounds of buoyancy an Extrasport Hi-Float provides.

On backcountry trips where any rational human being will go to any lengths to avoid a spill, a high-float jacket may seem like needless bulk; but because I assume that no matter how careful I am I just may screw up, I like that extra edge of safety the big jacket gives me. Imagine yourself on a cold, rainy day, clad in Bean boots, raingear, and multiple layers of wool. You're clambering around on slippery ledges, lining your boat down through deep, heavy water. You miss your footing and plop into the drink. If you're a bony, muscular type with all that cold- and foul-weather gear on, you probably weigh quite a bit more than ten or twelve pounds in the water, and that twenty-five pound tug up instead of down will feel awfully good. I can't speak for other heavy-water jackets, but the Extrasport Hi-Float is so well designed and cut that I have never felt hampered by it whether paddling, poling, or lining.

Buoyancy is just as crucial for the soul, of course, as it is for the body. You may survive a canoe journey well enough simply by keeping afloat physically, but if your spirits are sunk, you won't have much fun. Physical and spiritual buoyancy are intimately related because no one who is actually going under or who constantly feels in danger of going under is likely to be high-spirited. Anxiety is the great enemy of buoyancy. Anxiety weighs you down, and the only cure for it is competence. If you're confident of your canoecraft and campcraft, the prospect of some bugs, some wind, some rain, some wading and lining and portaging will not fill you with dread. You'll be free to relax, take in the glories around you, and ride all the waves of good talk, goofiness, and laughter that canoe trips seem to set rolling; and that in its turn will contribute to safety and comfort because happy people who are laughing a lot make better judgment calls than people who are grim, scared, or frantic. In the never-ending circle of things physical that affect things spiritual that affect things physical, competence contributes to good cheer which contributes to competence and so on.

Competence on an extended river trip is not a matter of hotshot whitewater skills alone but of good judgment, and good judgment is a distillate of a whole complex of skills both on the water and off. It requires not only the hands-on skills of canoeing, of navigation, of setting up a snug camp, of reading weather and water but also human savvy: having wits enough to stop and make hot soup for lunch before anyone gets too cold and grumpy, or to quit for the day rather than attempt one last rapid on everyone's last reserves of energy and attention.

That kind of judgment is one of the best life preservers you can find, and any canoe party in which it prevails is probably going to be as buoyant a company as they come.

CHURCHILL FALLS

THIS YEAR'S TRIP is over. Derek Morgan and his wife, Sondra, will drive us out the 115 miles of dirt road from Churchill Falls village to Esker, a whistle-stop on the Quebec North Shore and Labrador Railway. There we will load our outfit onto a southbound train that will take us back 286 miles to Sept Îles on the St. Lawrence where we left our cars over two weeks ago.

Our canoes are tied onto the racks of the pickup trucks, and we will take shifts riding in the cabs and the beds of the trucks. It's early September. White clouds, driven by a northwest wind, are scurrying across the huge, brilliantly blue sky of the Labrador plateau. Before too many more days have passed, there will be snow in the air. Those of us taking the first shift in the backs of the trucks will soon have to put on all the wool we have and then pull our raingear on over it to ward off, with only moderate success, the combined force of the wind in the air and the gale generated by the speed of the trucks.

But before we hunker down for that long, cold haul, we make a stop to visit what, for any river lover, has to be one of the saddest sights in North America. About twenty miles out of the village, the road crosses the river just above

31

Churchill Falls, and we pull into a gravel pit on the west end of the bridge. From there it is not far to the falls, a quarter mile maybe, certainly no more than a half. As we set out on the well-worn path we know what we are going to see; and if we had forgotten for a moment, the dry, silent jumble of massive rock under the two-hundred-yard span of the bridge serves as a reminder. We are going to pay our respects to the mortal remains of a great waterfall.

Until 1965, when both the river and the falls were renamed in honor of Winston Churchill, these falls were known as Grand Falls. Surely they had to be counted among the grandest falls of this continent or any other. With all due respect for Mr. Churchill and, for that matter, for Sir Charles Hamilton, the first colonial governor of Newfoundland whose name the river bore from 1821 until Churchill displaced him, I would submit that even the most powerful of politicians, when set side by side with this river, are mere twerps. The Grand River and its Grand Falls would be better served by the names the first explorers gave them.

Grandeur and beauty are inseparable in any great waterfall, but usually one quality or the other dominates. The world's very highest falls, which don't have large volumes of flow, are more beautiful than grand. Slim ribbons of water tumbling from high parapets, they have a delicacy about them that is often reflected in their names: Angel, Fairy, Bridalveil. They soar as in a swan dive, and as they drop one thousand or two thousand or three thousand feet, water dissipates into mist and cloud, like spirit freeing itself from flesh.

There is nothing ethereal about falls like Victoria and Churchill and Niagara. They measure only hundreds of feet in height, not thousands; but their volume is overwhelming. They come at you like a thundering herd, like elephants, buffalo, and longhorns combined, like the ride of the Valkyries. Where a ribbon of water cascading out of the sky seems a gift from some airy divinity, thirty- or forty- or fifty-thousand cubic feet of water per second roaring over a precipice and plunging into a canyon to boil and churn and smoke there inspire awe bordering on terror. The Indians of Labrador, understandably, gave the falls a wide berth; and their reluctance to go near either the falls or twelve-mile McLean Canyon below them—along with the incredible ruggedness of the Labrador interior—probably explains why so few white men ever reached Grand Falls until well into this century.

The number of recorded visits to the falls by whites in the 1800s can be counted on one hand, starting with John McLean of the Hudson's Bay Company in 1839. Another H.B.C. officer, named Kennedy, visited them again twenty years later; but the Bowdoin College expedition of 1891 was the first to photograph the falls and canyon and bring back even a rudimentary scientific description of them.

The construction first of the QNS and L Railway, built to bring out ore from the rich iron deposits of the central Quebec-Labrador peninsula, then of the haul road from Esker to the construction site of the Churchill Falls hydro-power plant changed all that. Churchill Falls did not become a tourist destination overnight, but it did become accessible to vastly larger numbers of people than it had ever been before. Edgar Corriveau, who runs an outfitting store in Sept Îles and who saw the falls before the power plant was completed, tells a story of what could happen to gawkers and camera clickers who lacked the Indians' piety. Two sightseers, he recounts, went out to the falls in the spring to photograph them at high water. Intent on getting dramatic shots, they ventured out onto some rocks near the brink of the falls. The rocks, continually drenched by the mist from the falls, still had a skim of ice on them. The two men slipped, fell, clutched frantically for handholds, slid into the water, and were instantly lost to sight. "They didn't stand a chance," Edgar said.

Perhaps understatement is the only way one can begin to hint at what those men's deaths must have been like, the consciousness, however briefly it lasted, of being a tiny speck of sentient life caught in the titanic grip of those falls where waters drawn from a 25,000-square-mile watershed are massed, squeezed together, and pushed through the eye of a needle to plunge some 250 feet into an immense scour basin the millennia have pummeled out of the rock below.

"Turbulence" is a phenomenon a physicist may analyze and experiment with, but the word doesn't begin to comprehend what went on at the foot of Churchill Falls, much less hint at what it would be like to experience it on one's own flesh. Yet I can't help wondering whether those two men didn't feel with their terror some lunatic exhilaration as well. Massive waterfalls inspire a dangerous, hypnotizing fascination in people, drawing them closer and closer to the edge and planting a question in the healthiest minds: "What *would* it be like to just step over?"

On that September afternoon when we visited the falls the answer was easy: It would have been like jumping into a rock pile. The river was dry, and at the falls only a pitiful dribble ran down the face of the rock. Churchill Falls had been reduced to a leaky faucet. There was no mist, no thundering roar. There was only the sound of the wind in the spruce. Austin Cary and Dennis Cole, the two men of the 1891 Bowdoin expedition who reached the falls, arrived there in late summer, too, and in what appears to have been an exceptionally dry year. But even so, the volume of the falls was so great that "the ground quaked with the shock of the descending stream."

Where has all that water gone? Now it is fodder for the eleven turbines of the Churchill Falls hydroelectric plant, one of the world's largest underground powerhouses with a generating capacity of 550 megawatts. But before it is sucked into the penstocks that will drop it about a thousand feet from the plateau down to the turbines and back into the river below McLean Canyon, it is stored in an immense reservoir. Unlike the American West, where hydropower storage is often accomplished by damming canyons and forming long, deep lakes, central Labrador is a huge tableland where water can be stored only by spreading it out, not by piling it up. Here, a system of low dikes built at strategic points has merged the great gangling lakes of the plateau—Lobstick, Michikamau, Windbound, Orma, Mackenzie, Vollant, and Kasheshibaw—into one huge beaver flowage a little over a third the size of Lake Ontario.

The day before our departure, we had toured the power plant that has drained Churchill Falls dry and put 2,700 square miles of Labrador under water. Newfoundland Hydro is proud of this plant, and even from people like me the place draws grudging admiration. It is something like the pyramids, a project so monumental in size and concept that one can't but respect the human ingenuity and sweat that went into it: the huge galleries blasted, bored, and chipped out of solid rock, the transport of the turbines that were designed so they would fit—with clearance of only a few inches—through the tunnels on the QNS and L. But, as with the pyramids, I also can't help asking: Is this something we really need? Granted, the Churchill Falls hydro-power plant was not bought with the human suffering that went into the pyramids, and it is presumably of benefit to humankind. Yet on some level I wonder if it is really of all that much greater benefit than a pyramid, if it too isn't as much a monument to the god-man of technology as the pyramids were to the god-man embodied in the pharaohs.

If Churchill Falls were the only project of its kind, we might be more inclined to give it the benefit of the doubt. But it seems instead to represent only one operation in an ongoing campaign to squeeze every last kilowatt out of the Quebec-Labrador peninsula. There is hardly a river in Labrador or Quebec that has not been surveyed for its hydropower potential, and the Lower Churchill Development Corporation, not content with Churchill Falls' 550 megawatts, is planning two more hydropower plants on the lower Churchill, a 618-megawatt station at Muskrat Falls and a 1,698-megawatt one at Gull Island Rapids, plants that will dwarf the giant already in place at Churchill Falls. If and when these plans are carried out, the Grand River will not be so grand any more.

And this is in Labrador alone, on one river alone, chicken feed next to the James Bay project in Quebec where "LG2," the largest underground powerhouse in the world, cranks out 5,238 megawatts on the La Grande River, where two other plants have capacities of 3,000 and 2,000 megawatts respectively, where hydropower reservoirs cover 4,600 square miles (not the mere 2,700 of Labrador's ironically

named Smallwood) with muck, stumps, and rapidly rising and falling waters, and where Phase 2 of the James Bay project is expected to raise total generating capacity to 25,000 megawatts.

We come back from our little detour to defunct Churchill Falls with no more factual information than we brought to it: We knew the falls were dead, but now that knowledge is visceral. The sight of death is different from the knowledge of it. Nobody can sing the praises of "clean" hydropower to me any more, and nobody can tell me that the loss of Churchill Falls is a fair price to pay to warm our water beds, run our video games, and light up our shopping malls.

COMFORT

AMONG THE MANY clippings in my mental scrapbook is an interview with Paul Petzold, the famed mountaineer and founder of the National Outdoor Leadership School based in Jackson, Wyoming. The occasion, the publication, all those details are lost to me now, but the gist of Petzold's remarks is not. He was arguing for a style of outdoor living and outdoor leadership training that stressed control, safety, and comfort, not uncertainty, risk, and hardship. His case, it seems to me, is irrefutable. Who, having gone on one or two or even several canoe trips or backpacking jaunts, will ever want to go again if he or she has spent most of the time wet, cold, hungry, exhausted, and terrified?

"Roughing it" has always struck me as a dumb phrase. It suggests that there is some kind of virtue in discomfort and inconvenience. Just get wet, cold, hungry, and exhausted enough, it says, and you will experience the true essence of the outdoors. Untrue. The only thing you'll experience is wet, cold, hunger, and exhaustion. You won't have any energy or attention left over to appreciate the flight of the kingfisher or the damp touch of the morning mist on your face or the raccoon tracks in the mud or any of the other little million things there are to attend to.

Every once in a while I wonder if my preoccupation with comfort isn't just a function of my graying head, my aging bones, and a wimpy nature. But then all I have to do is come across a party of wet, weary, ill-equipped young people to realize that misery knows no age limits. A tough, resilient youngster may be able to take more punishment than your average graybeard, but the young sufferer won't enjoy it any more than the old one will.

Comfort, like beauty, is its own excuse for being, but it has a practical function, too, because comfort is essential to safety. Paddlers who have not slept well for a week will not only be having a thoroughly lousy time, but they will also be functioning at less than optimum capacity. They will tend to make disastrous mistakes and then not have the physical reserves they need to pull themselves out of the messes they get into.

To sing the praises of comfort is not to say, however, that even careful management can make every minute of a canoe journey cushy. No such luck. Canoeing may be fun, but it is strenuous fun. It is always work and often very hard work. You may paddle under a pounding sun or buck a stiff headwind all day. With a canoe on your shoulders, you claw your way up and down hills through the brush, sometimes just for a few hundred yards, sometimes for miles. You pole upstream until your arms hang by your sides like last night's spaghetti. You go ashore for lunch and find you've picked the site of the Great North American Black-Fly Jamboree.

All that can still pass for fun if, at the end of the day, you can make a snug camp, eat a tasty, hearty meal, and crawl into a dry bed where no bugs can get at you. Being able to achieve that blessed state every night depends in large measure on having the right stuff and on knowing how to use it.

Volumes have been written on the right stuff and its use. I refer you to those volumes. All I want to do here is a little cheerleading for a couple of items that make outdoor living not just okay but shamelessly luxurious. High on my list, because I'm very fond of sleeping, is the Therm-a-Rest mattress. In pre-Therm-a-Rest days, there were air mattresses and foam pads. Air mattresses were of two kinds: the big, heavy rubberized canvas ones that took half an hour to inflate and just about as long to deflate (some folks found them quite comfortable as long as the night and the ground were not too cold) and the tiny, light ones that were easier to blow up but so skimpy that I always felt I was sleeping on a half-inflated basketball. At best, there's something disconcerting about sleeping on air trapped in a bunch of tubes. Squash it down here, and it bloops up there. If you're a restless sleeper an air mattress feels like a bad practical joke that lasts all night.

Open-cell foam pads were more comfortable if they were thick enough, but if they were that thick, they were a nuisance to pack and keep dry. Closed-cell foam insulated well and did not absorb water, but any pad thin enough to roll up into a packable bundle offered no more support for one's weary bones than a leftover flapjack would.

The Therm-a-Rest mattress is an open-cell foam pad with an air-tight skin bonded to the foam and a valve at one corner. In other words it is a cross between an air mattress and a foam pad, but it is far more than the sum of its parts. To pack it, you roll it up, squeezing as much air out of it as you can, then close the valve. In the evening, you just open the valve, and the mattress self-inflates in a few minutes. I always add a few puffs to firm it up before I close the valve. You're spared all that huffing and puffing that leaves you dizzy, and you've got a bed that is as close to cloud nine as I've ever come.

The standard Therm-a-Rest is one and a half inches thick and has a heavy nylon skin. For the last few years I've been using the Ultra Lite backpacker model, which is only an inch thick and has a much lighter nylon taffeta skin. You'd think that difference in thickness would make a huge difference in comfort, but it doesn't. Even on snow, cobblestone beaches, and the gnarliest of root systems the Ultra Lite has been an express magic carpet to dreamland. The standard model is obviously more durable, and the slight additional weight and bulk are no obstacle for a canoeist. If you want a Therm-a-Rest to double for both backpacking and canoeing, choose the Ultra Lite. It's tougher than it looks, and with reasonable care it will not let you down. Mine has sprung one easily repairable leak in four years of moderate use. Both models come in full or three-quarter length. If comfort is your goal, go full length. The third of you that is not on a shorty will complain so bitterly to the other two-thirds that none of you will be happy.

Is there anything wrong with the Therm-a-Rest? I've heard two complaints, neither of which have dampened my enthusiasm one whit. The first: The Therm-a-Rest is inflatable and therefore can have a blowout and therefore can let you down. The same can be said of pneumatic tires. I'll carry a repair kit and take my chances. The second: The Therm-a-Rest is expensive. Both the standard and the Ultra Lite cost fifty dollars in the full-length models. Granted, that's more money than fifteen dollars for a superlight backpacker air mattress or twenty dollars for a foam pad; but it's still only half what a fancy motel room would cost you, and if I used my Therm-a-Rest only one night a year, I'd still think the money well spent.

The only thing I find puzzling about the reception of the Therm-a-Rest is the restraint with which its adherents speak of it. In his *Song of the Paddle* the great Bill Mason simply called it "the best choice of mattress." Colin Fletcher, the dean of backpackers, gives it the clear nod but at no time indulges in language more excessive than calling the three-quarter-length Ultra Lite "a little gem."

The Therm-a-Rest wakens more than mere enthusiasm in me. It touches me where I really live. It moves me to sing its praises, to wax poetic. With deep devotion and gratitude, I offer this humble haiku:

> Therm-a-Rest, my love,
> Flat as the sea. I float on
> Your foamy bosom.

What else is essential to comfort? Well, an axe, I think. A real one. Not a hatchet, but an axe long enough and heavy enough to retain some authority when swung with two hands yet light enough not to wipe out your wrist if you use it one-handed to split out kindling or slice branches off firewood poles. I use an ancient, forge-welded three-pound axe with a twenty-eight-inch handle. If I didn't already own this one, I'd buy a two-and-a-half-pound axe with a twenty-eight-inch handle from Snow and Nealley in Bangor, Maine. That's still heavy enough to do anything I ever want to do on a canoe trip, and I know my wrist would appreciate eight ounces less for one-handed work.

The major argument the anti-axe contingent comes up

with is safety: "You'll lop your own feet off way out in the woods somewhere, and then won't you be in a sorry pickle." That would be an embarrassment, and anyone who feels it's a real possibility for him should put in a lot of practice with an ambulance standing by before he heads into the bush, axe in hand.

But for the experienced axe handler, the tool's benefits far outweigh its risks. In the normal run of camp life it provides easy access to firewood, and after days of drenching rain about the only tinder and kindling you'll be able to find is what you can split out of the heart of sound deadwood. Being able to build a fire quickly is always a comfort, and it can be essential to safety as well. In the northern forest where the water is always cold and where rain, wind,

and low air temperatures often create ideal conditions for hypothermia, an axe is your only guarantee of a dependable fuel supply. To my mind, if wood is readily available, it's folly *not* to carry an axe, and an axe is about the last thing I would ever want to be without.

In addition to being your fuel maker, it cuts poles for your cooking crane and shear poles for stringing a rain tarp. If you break your setting pole, you can cut and smooth a new one with your axe. If you break a paddle, you can make a new one with an axe. If you burn up your Therm-a-Rest mattress, you can cut boughs for a bed with your axe. With an axe, you can build shelters ranging from lean-tos to log cabins. In short, there's not much in the way of providing comforts and necessities that you can't do with an axe. Mention "comfort" and the mind turns automatically to shelter from the wind and rain, dry boots, warm clothes, and soft, warm beds. Nobody is inclined to cuddle up to a hunk of cold, sharp steel. But an axe in every boat, plus someone who knows how to use it, is one of the greatest sources of creature comfort any canoe trip can have.

CUTTING THE UMBILICAL CORD

ON THE LAST day or two before I leave for a canoe trip I realize just how ironlike and weblike is the fabric of my everyday life, and the longer the trip will be, the stronger and tighter that weave seems. Last-minute preparations for the trip are the least of my worries, little jobs like sharpening my axe, putting fresh Sno-Seal on my Bean boots, revarnishing my favorite paddle, or buying some new wool socks. If I will be away three weeks or a month, the work that would normally be done in that time has to be done ahead, so, first of all, there is the scramble to get everything written for the deadlines that will fall during my resounding absence.

And there are the long-undone chores that have to be done now, not later. The electric fence around the garden, for example, has to be fixed *now* in early August, or the raccoons will eat corn for the rest of August while I'm gone, and I won't eat any in September when I get back. That is no small matter. I love fresh corn straight out of the garden.

I have to see that my wife, Rita, has enough kindling and summer wood to last for three weeks.

I have to change the oil in the car, sharpen the lawnmower blade, finally write that letter to a long-lost high-school friend who sent me a Christmas card last year, who is now living in Hawaii, whom I haven't seen for thirty years, and whom I never really liked all that much in the first place.

The reality is, of course, that all these last-minute details I feel compelled to deal with don't have to be dealt with at all. The car won't fall apart in the next five hundred miles if its oil isn't changed. The lawnmower, which has been operating at less than peak efficiency all summer, can muddle through for another mowing or two. Old Charlie out there on Oahu will not languish and expire if he doesn't hear from me in the next week. Rita is plenty adept with an axe and would never lack for kindling if a UFO abducted me tomorrow. Even the corn isn't *that* important.

So why do I put myself through this? Why do I stay up until all hours before a trip dispatching a lot of trivia? Why am I still stumbling around outside at 1:00 A.M. with a headlamp, running a last strand of electric-fence wire around the garden?

The reason is, I think, because any extended wilderness canoe journey is a crossing over Jordan, a passage from one life to another, a leaving the cozy, comfy, constricting womb of the everyday to venture out into you-don't-know-quite-what; and whenever we human beings feel we are about to leave one world for another—whether to pass from life to death or, less drastically, to move from one continent to another or even just from Albany, New York, to Keokuk, Iowa—we feel compelled to wrap up loose ends and put our houses in order. If I really thought I'd cross over Jordan on a canoe trip, I wouldn't go. But even when I walk out the door fully confident that I'll walk back in again, I know that I'm heading for territories, physical and spiritual, that neither I nor most so-called civilized people, no matter how "rural" our lives, do not ordinarily inhabit.

For the Iatmul people of Papua New Guinea, the canoe is a link between the natural and supernatural worlds. Symbolic carvings of canoes manned by spirit figures are used in ceremonies of initiation and of communication with the dead, and I'm sure if I knew more about canoe mythology and lore around the world, there'd be many more examples of this kind to cite. At any rate, I know what the Iatmul are talking about. I know that the deeper and farther I paddle a canoe into realms still largely untouched by industrial man, the deeper I am immersed in a world not supernatural but one in which nature is still fully itself, undiluted and undiminished by the overlay of our inhuman human presence. I don't see or sense anything above, below, or beyond nature. I simply see more of the spectrum, more of what nature is that I just haven't seen before.

Traveling wild country in a canoe is like leaving a house to go outdoors. Instead of seeing only what you can see through a window, you can now see in all directions, north, south, east, and west, up into the heavens and down into the depths. You don't just see; you also hear, smell, and feel on your skin. Instead of seeing just one square foot of the canvas, you see the whole painting. And seeing more, you want to see still more yet. Your hunger grows, and so you go back again and again. You go more often and stay longer.

I haven't seen any ghosts. I haven't had any visions, but on my limited sorties into the bush, I get inklings of dimensions that are closed to me in the normal rounds of my experience, not inklings of "other" worlds but of the height and depth and breadth of this one here under my feet. In *True North*, Elliott Merrick's account of the winter of 1930–31 he spent traveling with the trappers of Labrador, there are innumerable passages at once down-to-earth and lyrical that reflect just what it is that makes anyone once bitten by the North keep going back for more. After a couple of brutally hard days hauling toboggans down the Grand River on the ice in early January, Merrick, his wife, Kay, and John Michelin sank down exhausted by their campfire on Mininipi Island, and Merrick wrote:

> Oh, the happiness that fills us is as strong and quiet as Grand River. Just as the river never stops flowing down under the ice, so this ecstasy will flow forever in our hearts, carrying us with it to a limitless sea of hope and understanding and sympathy. In this life where one can conceal nothing, not even from oneself, it seems we have found ourselves out for the first time, found what we really are and what living is. It is like getting to the bottom of things, as though from this as a starting point we could live true. . . . Last night I thought this life was a brutalizing ordeal, a long, long

49

chain of pain that one numbed oneself to endure. Tonight I think that we have touched the earth's core and found meaning. Whatever it is we sought, we have found. We hold it in our hands, dreaming by the fire.

I've never come near to traveling as far and deep and hard as Merrick did, but I've traveled just far and deep and hard enough to sense what he is talking about, to know what it is like to at least reach out for the earth's core. And whenever people set out on journeys like that, it's not surpising that a little prying and wrenching takes place, for no matter how much we want to go, there's also a reluctance to leave the safe and familiar and a need to build a lot of last-minute bridges back to our old terra firma, hence the frantic attending to chores that could be put off. We somehow feel if we've done right on our way out, the gods will let us come back. Each chore done is a little bridge back to our comfortable reality.

The other form this reluctant eagerness to leave takes is in all the stops one makes en route to the put-in, food stops, pit stops, equipment stops, stops that combine two or possibly all three of those functions. If I were the only person I knew who indulged in this behavior, I'd think it a personal oddity. But just about everyone I've ever traveled with participates in it to some degree.

Food purists who normally would never dream of stopping at a McDonald's will scream out "Golden Arches! Coffee stop!" in such unlikely places as Millinocket, Maine, or Sainte-Marie de Beauce or Baie Comeau, Quebec (Yes, Virginia, there is a McDonald's in Baie Comeau). Almost everyone has either forgotten some small item or planned to pick it up along the way—extra flashlight batteries, toothpaste, a new fly line, some leaders—and so we stop at the big general store on top of Indian Hill in Greenville. And even if you go into the store not planning to buy anything, you usually do, even if it's just a couple of postcards that you scribble hasty messages on and drop off at the post office on the way out of town, messages that say, no matter what else they say, "I'm off beyond the reach of telephones and radios. I'm lost to this world, but please don't forget me while I'm gone."

On Route 138 that takes us all the way from Quebec City to Sept Îles there are special stops that have acquired the status of roadside shrines, places where we stop not just to eat or camp but also to commune briefly with our pagan saints of the road and ask their blessing. The little village of Les Escoumins rims a deep, protected bay where, on calm summer nights, the boats in the harbor seem afloat on liquid glass. And even if it were not time for supper, which it almost always is when we arrive at Les Escoumins, we would at least stop for tea at Restaurant Le Petit Régal, whose windows overlook the bay and the comings and goings of seagulls.

And so it goes all the way to Sept Îles and until the very moment we board the QNS and L to head north into the bush. There is a special spot on the beach between Baie-des-Bacons and Sault-au-Mouton, two tiny towns I like to think of as the Bay of Pigs and Sheep's Leap, where we always pull off to camp for the night. There is a special restaurant in Forestville where we always stop for French toast. Lunch has to be bought in the Provigo store in Port-Cartier and include, if nothing else, roasted chickens packed in foil-lined bags, chickens we usually scarf down in the shopping center parking lot.

51

In Sept Îles our fellow paddler Kimberly wants to be sure she gets a manuscript sent off to her agent before the post office closes. I stop at a drugstore for sunglasses and Tums. I hardly ever have an upset stomach, but just in case. Even as I buy it, I know the roll of Tums is a hedge against the unforeseen and the unforeseeable, a talisman, not a necessity. It, like the too many extra pens and notebooks I always have with me, is one more link in that chain that binds me to my old, safe routines. If I live long enough, I think, I may really be able to trim my kit down to the true necessities. If I live long enough and can learn enough, I may someday be ready to set off into the bush with an axe, a shotgun, raingear, one change of clothes, matches, a knife, some flour and tea. And by the time the clothes and the raingear are worn out, the matches and the shotgun shells and the flour and the tea long gone, I won't need them anymore.

But as it is, I drag my umbilical cord behind me as a diver does his air line. I'm not able and therefore not ready to cut myself altogether free, and all the little rituals and treats that I and others enjoy so much on the way to the edge of our Jordan and some of which I pack up and take along with me remind me that I'm still a long way from the core of the earth, a long way from those paths and waterways the Cree, the Montagnais, and the Iatmul of New Guinea have been traveling for millennia.

*E*FFICIENCY APARTMENT

SOMETIMES IT RAINS. Hard. And long. Often there are bugs, zillions of them. Sometimes it snows. If you're not prepared for those eventualities, which are inevitabilities at the appropriate times of year, you're in for some misery.

Anyone who travels in bug country in the summer will have foresight enough to carry a tent that not only sheds rain effectively but also excludes all attacking insects, no matter how small they may be. Where no-see-ums threaten, that means a tent with netting fine enough to exclude those fiendish, microscopic little creatures. No-see-um netting creates some minor discomfort because it restricts air flow and creates some weird visual effects. A full moon viewed through it takes on some unmoonlike colors—blues, greens, purples. But for relief from no-see-ums and from the dismal alternative of drenching yourself and your sleeping bag with bug dope for the night, I'll gladly put up with some stuffiness and a blue moon.

But bug- and rainproof sleeping quarters take care of only part of your dwelling problems. No less important is having a place to get out of the rain at mealtimes, a place where you can cook, eat, and lounge around in comfort despite a persistent nor'easter. For much of the canoeing season, that means

a rain tarp, which can be set up in any number of configurations—lean-to, gable roof, you name it—depending on wind
and weather and whatever is or is not available to hitch it to.
Where trees are plentiful, a little geometrical thinking and an
ample supply of light rope and parachute cord will often let
you set up your tarp without supplying any structural mem-
bers at all. Where natural growth is not so cooperative, you
can lash four canoe poles together into two sets of shear poles
and stretch a ridge line between the shears to suspend your
tarp on.

A rain tarp can make all the difference between a sodden,
demoralized trip and one where you can sit back and enjoy
the warmth of your fire and the patter of rain overhead, not
into your plate. On a recent Gaspé trip that began on a day of
heavy, nonstop rain, a member of our party unaccustomed to
the blessings of a rain tarp insisted on putting up his tent and
crawling into it the instant we quit for the day.

"In weather like this," he said, "all I want to do is hole up."

The rest of us, using two sets of shear poles, set up the rain
tarp on the scrubby little island where we were camping, got a
fire going, started some potatoes baking, and just before the
steaks and the asparagus were done, we coaxed our rain-weary
friend out of his tent for a tot of Jim Beam. The minute he
saw that there was a fire going, food on the way, some good
whiskey in sight, and—more important still—a dry place to
enjoy it all, the expression on his face was instantly transformed from gloom to good cheer.

Many campers and canoeists use 4- or 6-mil plastic sheeting
for rain tarps. It is cheap and easily replaceable, and used with
Visklamps, which can be hooked into it at any point you like,
it can be rigged in just about any configuration the human
mind might devise.

54

Personally, I detest the damn stuff. It's slippery and slithery; it rattles unpleasantly in the wind; and the Visklamps operate on the same principle as garter clamps, which I have always regarded as the world's most decadent and unecessarily complex way to hold up socks or stockings. Plastic sheeting is also extremely prone to tears and punctures, and so one's rain tarp is soon a candidate for the landfill.

The most popular alternative is lightweight coated nylon, which is more pleasant to handle and has a longer life expectancy, though one could object that it, too, is non-biodegradable. Even better from both an aesthetic and environmental point of view is lightweight, high-count cotton. The initial price is daunting, but properly cared for, the cotton will outlast any other fabric and ultimately be the most economical choice.

What's the ideal size? I don't know, though I do know that no matter how large a tarp is, it could always be larger when I'm under it, and when it's time to pack it, it could always be smaller. The one I use most is ten by twelve feet, which is quite adequate for a party of four. For larger groups, two eight-by-tens can yield more versatile setups than one monstrous circus tent that can't be snugged into spruce woods without clearing half an acre first.

When the cold autumn rains, the sleet, and the early wet snows start to fall, it's time to retire the summer tents and tarps and carry an eight-by-ten or ten-by-twelve cotton wall tent and a small sheet-steel stove. The heated wall tent has been the traditional shelter of the Canadian north woods for generations, and there is nothing like it for sheer luxury. You come in off the river late on a cold, rainy, windy afternoon feeling half hypothermic even if you aren't, but once you have the tent up, some wood split, and a fire crackling away in the stove, the whole aspect of the world changes. Within minutes, you're peeling off layers, expanding in the heat, putting on water for a quick cup of tea before you settle in to the serious business of getting supper.

If you've taken on a couple of bootfuls of water, you change into dry socks and sneakers, hang your wet socks on the line along the ridgepole, and invert your boots over a few stakes driven into the ground close enough to the stove to get some heat but not so close you melt your boots. By morning your footgear will be blissfully dry.

As darkness comes on, you drive a couple more stakes into the ground and tie candles to them with light wire. By now the temperature in the tent is about seventy, and you're down to your underwear shirt. The wind goes on blowing, the rain keeps raining; you could care less. You're not outside trying to cook over a wind-tossed and rain-spattered fire by the light of a headlamp, your back hunched to the wind, your jacket pulled up around your ears.

Inside the tent, the level of comfort is so overwhelming that you can forget what a filthy night it is outside, so it's a good idea, in the interest of keeping a realistic perspective on things, to step outdoors occasionally for a bracing slap of rain in the face. It makes you appreciate just how good you've got it. And if you wander out on the caribou moss a ways and turn to look back at the tent glowing from the light of the candles within, it seems, in the vast blackness of the Canadian night, like a tiny wayside shrine in which the votive lamp never goes out. The pilgrims inside aren't saying any prayers, of course. They're boiling a duck, sipping a dash of rum, wiggling their toes in the heat of the stove, telling stories on each other and themselves, cackling, chortling, and rolling around on the floor in total weeping hysteria if the stories get good enough. The tone may be a little too boisterous for proper vespers, but what I hear rising from the warmth and light of that tent is an evensong as full of good tidings as any mortal could hope for.

$\mathcal{F}$IRE

THE REASON WHY all books about canoeing and camping have a section about fire in them isn't because building fires is such a complicated business that it has to be explained over and over again or that any author who writes about it has such novel ideas on the subject that the world has to hear them. The reason is that no one ever seems to outgrow the desire to light matches and play with fire, and what's fun to do is usually fun to write about, too.

In dry weather, building fires is gratifyingly easy. You just twist a bunch of twiggy, bone-dry fuzz off a dead spruce, mush it into a ball, stick a match under it, drop it on the ground, and start leaning kindling into the flames. Within minutes the tea water is boiling, and if you're a little paddle- and bone-weary, life suddenly looks much brighter again.

In a cold drizzle or a driving downpour, building a fire is probably even more fun, both because the challenge is so much greater and the comfort obtained so much more appreciated. If somebody in your party is shivering violently and on the brink of hypothermia, then fun be damned. All you want to do is get the furnace roaring. Against such an occasion, I always have a plastic bag with a fist-sized gob of birch bark and a little bundle of short cedar splits in it tucked away in my day pack. I started doing that after I read about a canoe party in Ontario that had been so desperately in need of fire on a cold, wet day that they chopped and shaved a wooden paddle into tinder and kindling. There are plenty of crummy wooden paddles that deserve to go that route, but mine are not among them. I've never felt—yet—the need to dig into my emergency tinder, but it's reassuring to have it.

In the normal, nonemergency situation, you can take your time and enjoy the game of fire building. First comes the treasure hunt, the search for sound, standing deadwood that, when split open, will yield dry shavings and kindling no matter how drenched the outside may be. In regions where it grows, white cedar is what every rainy-day canoeist hopes to find close to camp. Dead cedar burns hot and clean, and the wood is so soft that with a sharp pocket knife you can peel a mound of paper-thin shavings off it in a very few minutes. The shavings roll away from the blade with a whispering, ripping sound that presages the warm voice of the fire.

Lacking cedar, you make do with what you can find—spruce, fir, whatever. But whatever you make your shavings of, they have to be scrupulously isolated from moisture, as if they would melt if they so much as looked at a drop of water. You cannot let them fall onto the soggy ground and lie there. You cannot be dripping water on them from your hat or the sleeves of your raingear. In a sea of slop you have to create a mini-Sahara and keep your tinder as crisp as a fresh potato chip. Under the rain tarp, your wet sleeves rolled back, you can slice shavings off into a wanigan or your hat, anyplace to keep them out of the wet and damp.

When you have your glob of tinder and have split a

mound of kindling down so small you can't fit an axe into it any more and have twice as much pencil-sized and thumb-sized wood as you can possibly use and three times as much full-sized firewood as you would use on a dry day, then, and only then, is it time to touch a match to your ball of tinder and lay your infant flame down on a manger of bark or dry splits. Then it is time to nurture it, feeding it shavings, toothpicks, splinters, adding more and more solid food to its mother's milk as it grows and flourishes, bouncing and leaping and filling your fond parental heart with warmth and glee.

In spells of extended bad weather when it pours all day and pours all night and you leave a sodden camp in the morning and set up a drenched one again in the evening, you can save yourself a lot of fuss by carrying the eternal

flame along. You don't have to go so far as poor Cro-
Magnon did and actually pack away some smoldering moss.
All you need to do is pack away a reasonable supply of tinder and kindling in the wanigan when you break camp in
the morning. From one oasis of warmth and dryness, you
carry the makings of the next one. In fire building, anticipation is all.

$\mathcal{F}$ IRST RIVER

I WISH I could say I was born and raised on the banks of
the Nahanni or the Yukon or the Mackenzie. I wish I could
say, like Romulus and Remus, that I was suckled by wolves,
that my first teddy bear was a live grizzly, that at the age of
three I made my first solo trip across the Barren Grounds
from Great Slave Lake to Chesterfield Inlet and that in the
intervening years I pioneered routes on the White Nile, the
Blue Nile, and the Tunguska of central Siberia. With that
kind of pedigree I could say anything I liked about rivers
and canoes, and everyone would believe me, even if what I
said was the purest drivel.

Even being born and raised on the banks of the Allagash
would lend a little authority and panache, but I can't claim
even that. My first river was no wild, raging monster of the
Northwest Territories, nor even a friendly little fifty-mile
creek tucked away amidst the pulp plantations of Maine. It
was the Rockaway River of northern New Jersey, a poor,
insignificant, suburban worm of a river that rises somewhere, I believe, up near the Morris and Sussex County
line. It flows through Wharton and Rockaway, little towns
my high school used to play in football. I can't trace the
whole course of the Rockaway in my mind. I never attempt-

ed to put a boat in at the top of it and run down to its confluence with the Passaic. My acquaintance with it was piece-
meal, the stretch of it I knew best bracketed between the
towns of Denville and Boonton.

Just east of Denville the river is flat and slow. Some wil-
lows grow along its banks, and on the north side is a large
field the nuns in the St. Francis Convent used to till. The
nuns' field was at the head of the Rockaway valley, the first
of several rich, truck-farming fields along the meandering
course of the river between Denville and Boonton six or
seven miles downstream. Just below the convent, the river
swings north and bisects the golf course of the Rockaway
River Country Club. The river constitutes a major hazard
on this golf course and—for caddies with a little spare time
on their hands—a source of extra income.

I won't say that the majority of the RRCC's golfers were
duffers in the years I caddied there, but an inordinately high
number of golf balls that were supposed to go winging
across the Rockaway River wound up sliced or dubbed into
it. On a Monday morning after a weekend of heavy play, a
caddy could wade into the river and, by exploring the bottom with his bare feet, harvest a sizable crop of lost balls,
which he could then sell to golfers as practice balls. My
friend John Miller had toes long and agile enough that he
could pick up golf balls with them. Less talented, I could
locate the balls with my feet but then had to dive to pick
them up with my hands. It wasn't as profitable as pearl diving, but a buck was a buck.

We never paddled a canoe on the Rockaway, but it gave
us our first lessons in river navigation anyhow. The current
was steady and persistent but never so strong that it would
sweep us away if we waded waist, belly, or even chest deep.

We could probe the bottom with our feet, then lift them, give our weight to the water, and let it carry us a few yards downstream. Floating on our backs, we could do lazy ferrying maneuvers to shift ourselves back and forth across the current. We could skim by a big midstream rock, catch the eddy, and hang motionless in the rock's shelter. Plying the Rockaway for golf balls we learned basic river tactics literally on our own hides.

The other stretch of the Rockaway we came to know as well, if not better, than the road to school was the half mile just below the Powerville dam in Boonton. In the hundred-yard riffle below the dam and in the big slow pools below that the state fish and game department poured thousands of liver-fed trout; and on April 15, opening day of fishing season, the banks and shallows of the Rockaway were mobbed with elbow-to-elbow fishermen. John Miller and I were among them. More importantly, we were back the next day after school. And the day after that. We were back when

nobody else was back and when the population of liver-feds had been so decimated that we had to work hard to hook one or two. Instead of probing the bottom for golf balls, we learned where scarce trout were likely to lie and learned how to drift a worm into eddies and the pockets behind rocks so that not even a smart trout would know a line was attached to it.

But, of course, the river yielded far more to us than hard little balls that could be traded for dollars, more than tactical lessons, more than our share of hatchery trout. We learned, as Heraclitus had learned centuries ago, that it is impossible to step into the same river twice. The river is permanent yet constantly rising, falling, shifting, slipping away. We learned —as we probed the rich muck with our toes or explored the movements of currents and the lairs of fish with our worms and, later, our nymphs and wet flies—that the river was at once teeming with life and the tomb of the life it spawned. It smelled sweet and clean after a spring shower; on steamy days in August its backwaters and bogans stank of marsh gas and rotting fish.

Long before we learned what metaphors were we had learned that the river was no mere metaphor for life. It was the real thing. It was a vein carrying the earth's lifeblood, just as our veins carried our lifeblood. Our blood is 97 per-cent water, flowing from our hearts to our toes and back again. Water flowing from the snowmelt in the mountains through the capillaries of brooks and streams finds its way back to the heart of the sea, is lifted into the air, falls on the mountains as snow and rain, and flows back to the sea again. The river brings nourishment and carries away wastes. It bounds and leaps and cavorts; it is sullen; it plods on; it takes to its heels. It is the very image of us and our very substance. Without water there would be no plants, no animals, no us.

Our love of water is instinctive and visceral. We know we need to drink quart upon quart upon quart of it every day to survive in either the heat or the cold. It is the one true elixir of life. Adam's ale, my old friend Don Yeaton called it. Water can easily be our death, but without it neither we nor the planet can live, and it requires only a minor leap of the imagination to see the river as our blood brother and sister, flowing water as our mother and father. To travel the river and fish in its waters is to live so much at one with unexplained mystery and miracle that we feel no need of explanation.

So the Rockaway was not the Nahanni, the Yukon, the Mackenzie, or even the Allagash. It didn't need to be. It didn't teach me everything I wanted to know and needed to know and still haven't learned yet, but it gave me and taught me plenty. It was a first love. I went home from it with its perfumes in my nostrils and its voice in my ear. It roused a hunger in me that cannot, I suppose, be called sexual but that is surely erotic, a hunger that can never be stilled, no matter how often it is sated. I have gone back to the river again and again and will continue to go for as long as I can walk or crawl. And for the gift of that hunger I remain eternally grateful to the little Rockaway.

ℱLEECE AND WOOL

TIMES WERE WHEN fleece was what came off of sheep and was spun into woolen yarn. Now if you say fleece, folks may think you're talking about a soft, thick polyester material that is often marketed under fancy names like Polarpuff or Plasticfluff. Synthetic piles and fleeces have taken the outdoor-clothing field by storm, and you'll be hard-pressed to find much wool left in many upscale, outdoorsy catalogs. Fortunately for us old wool-gathering and wool-loving curmudgeons, there's still plenty of good wool clothing around, manufactured by Pendleton, Woolrich, Johnson Woolen Mills, and that builder of the ultimate in heavyweight wool, the C. C. Filson Company of Seattle.

For all but some special circumstances, which I will mention shortly, wool is superior to the synthetics. It is nowhere near as bulky; it doesn't melt if a spark lands on it; it grows on sheep, not in oil wells; and it provides a snug, animal warmth that I have never experienced in a synthetic garment.

But to give the synthetics their due, they do have one great virtue: they are hydrophobic. Because the synthetic fibers absorb next to no water, simply shaking out a drenched garment will rid it of much water. The garment will then will then dry faster than wool, which does absorb a lot of water and, depending on the thickness of the fabric, can take a long time to dry. But useful as that hydrophobic property can be, it has seduced the promoters of synthetics into some extravagant claims. The conventional advertising wisdom about underwear made of polyester or polypropylene is that it "wicks moisture away from your skin" and into your next layer of clothing where, presumably, it evaporates. The upshot of this wicking miracle is that you are supposed to remain dry and therefore warm. In my own humble experience, that has proved to be stark, raving nonsense.

If I (foolishly) work myself into a sweat in cold weather, I've overcome the ability of my clothes to release as vapor the amount of perspiration I'm putting out, and whether I have on wool, polypropylene, or chain-mail underwear won't matter a whit. If I slow down and ventilate my clothes enough so that my body heat can start drying out my soggy underwear, the synthetic may dry out somewhat sooner than wool; but as evaporation proceeds, it will cool me off, and I'll still be wet, cold, and miserable, perhaps dangerously so, for a long time. The only way, in other words, to stay warm and dry is not by relying on any miracle wicking fabric but by peeling off layers before you start to sweat, no matter what fabric you're wearing.

So should the canoe traveler just forget about synthetics, both in underwear and in insulating garments, and rely entirely on wool? No, I don't think so. Because I find wool much more comfortable and because my own tripping style is conservative enough to keep me out of cold water, I wear wool almost all the time in cool weather. But for those occasions when there is no way to avoid being drenched repeatedly for many hours at a time, I carry a set of lightweight polypropylene underwear, a fleece jacket, and a pair of fleece pants.

It would seem that only a madman would ever get himself into a situation where repeated dunkings are inevitable, but it can happen to the sanest of canoeists. The Bonaventure River on the Gaspé, for instance, rises in a couple of tiny ponds in the Chic-Choc Mountains and is a small, winding mountain stream for its first four or five miles. It then disappears into a huge flowage in which progress is blocked by downed trees at every turn. Navigating this mess calls for wading and wallowing, moosing canoes over blowdowns, chopping branches away so that you can slide a boat through underneath, grunting, groaning, and hauling and spending the best part of a day up to your knees, waist, and armpits in very cold water.

For this passage, I wore the synthetic fleece with my raingear over it. In the water, the fleece provided some measure of insulation, and when I climbed up and out between dunkings, the synthetic fabric quickly dumped the water it had taken on, leaving only the cuffs of the pants sodden. The raingear over the damp but still functioning insulating layer helped keep my body heat in. Considering that it was early June and not that long after ice-out, I stayed amazingly comfortable.

So my own conclusion is to use a mixed bag made up of mostly wool with one set of water-shedding, quick-drying, oil-well clothes, both underwear and insulating layer, for situations like the boglands of the upper Bonaventure. For the other 98 percent of my time on the river, I'll rejoice in the cozy company of my wool.

$\mathcal{H}$OSTILE WINDS

WIND MAY WELL be the most dangerous and terrifying of elemental forces a canoeist faces. A woman who has spent a fair amount of her adult life in a canoe once said to me, "It's not the monster rapids that scare me. You can always get off a river. It's those big expanses of open water that give me the heebie-jeebies." What she meant was open water with gale force winds whipping across it. Once you're a couple of miles out in a big lake you can't just "get off." And if it's a big lake right after ice-out when the water temperature is about thirty-eight degrees or a subarctic lake where the water temperature is always about thirty-eight degrees, an extended dip means you're dead meat.

Much of the time you can hug a shore or wiggle along among islands that can provide a haven in time of need. But at some point, to avoid paddling fifteen miles around a shoreline, you'll have to make a crossing of two or three miles or more. You hope you can make those crossings on misty, windstill days, and if you can't, you get up before dawn and cross before the sun and the wind come up. Or you wait until the wind dies in the evening.

But sometimes you do something stupid. About the scaredest I think I've ever been in a canoe was just below

70

Muskrat Falls on the Churchill River in Labrador. We'd just carried around the falls on a hot day in August, and the flies had massacred us on the portage. We couldn't wait to get out of their clutches, and we paddled out into the open water, heading across a large bay in the lakelike bulge of the river. Behind us, black clouds were building, and if we took any cognizance of them at all, it was only to say to ourselves, "We'll be across long before they catch up with us."

How wrong we were. The squall swept across the water like a huge hand sweeping plates off a table. I was paddling solo and had my boat trimmed stern heavy to keep it tracking in the slight tail wind we'd had all day. So suddenly did the wind rise that it didn't even lift any waves. It just riffled the surface of the water, slammed into my canoe with an audible whack, and spun the boat broadside. Instead of broaching in the water, I was broaching in the wind, and as in a broach, the wind, like the current, seemed intent on sucking my "upstream" gunwale under water and rolling the canoe over.

Just a week earlier, when we'd arrived in Churchill Falls to begin our trip, we'd met the local constable as he was about to transport a dead man to the morgue in Goose Bay. The man had been fishing on the river and had drowned when, as everyone told us, his "canoe blew over." I remember thinking how odd that was. A canoe might tip or swamp in heavy waves, but "blow over"?

Now I was finding out just how accurate that language was. This wind seemed strong enough to flip my canoe end over end and fling me out of it like a stone from a slingshot. I backpaddled as hard as I could to bring the stern up into the wind and give the wind less of a target. I put all my weight and strength into the strokes but couldn't break the

71

boat loose from that hand that was swiping it sideways, threatening to roll it and send me on a lethal swim. The only other boat in our party that was within shouting distance of me was in as much trouble as I was and couldn't be counted on for help.

I didn't even dare take the time to turn around, kneel, and gain the power advantage a forward stroke would give me. If I had my paddle out of the water that long and couldn't lean on it for that split second, I felt I would surely go over.

For however many minutes or seconds it took me to win control of the boat—thanks either to my own frantic efforts or an infinitesimal abatement in the wind or both—I thought I was a dead duck.

But once I had breathing space to turn and kneel, the possibility of survival looked a little brighter. In that more powerful position, I could keep the canoe into the wind, and I could also see a small rockpile of an island that my friends were inching their way toward.

Soon both our boats were in the lee of it. We beached them, then climbed up onto the rocks with binoculars to see if our companions in the three canoes ahead of us had made it to shore safely. We could count three boats and six heads, and we could see that they had their glasses up and were counting the three of us as eagerly as we were counting them.

The squall passed as quickly as it had come up, and we were soon able to set off on gently rippling water to rejoin our group. Safely reunited, we all vowed that until we made our next big mistake, we would never do anything that stupid again.

$\mathcal{U}$NJUSTICE

THE GUIDEBOOKS CALL Big Black Rapids on the St. John River in Maine Class II, not very serious stuff as rapids go; but still, on a remote river trip, it's wise to be prepared for the mistake you don't expect to make. So just above the rapids, George Dennison and I pulled into the bank to stuff any loose odds and ends into packs and make sure everything was tied into the boat snugly. As we were tying our last knots, we saw a slight, gray-templed man paddling solo in a short aluminum canoe come around the big bend above the rapids. The prospect of a river full of whitewater in front of him didn't faze the man at all. He made no move to pull ashore and scout. He made not the slightest adjustment in his approach but seemed to be precisely where he wanted to be in the river, right on the line he meant to take into and through the rapids, like a pilot glued onto his radar signal.

We watched, impressed, as the little canoe dropped into the whitewater, drifting effortlessly down the cleanest possible route. Utterly relaxed, the paddler sculled his paddle gently, keeping his boat under firm but easy control.

"That guy must know this river like the back of his hand," George said.

"Yeah," I agreed. "He came around that bend right in the

74

groove. It's nice to watch somebody who really knows what he's doing."

"It sure is," George said.

With that exchange, we climbed back into our boat, ferried out about a third of the way across the river from the left bank, and headed on down. Our run was not as elegant as our predecessor's had been. We had to lean hard on our paddles a few times, but we came through without any bumps or scrapes and drifted on down to the campsite at the confluence of the Big Black River and the St. John to stop for a little lunch.

The paddler of the little aluminum canoe had pulled in there for the same purpose. After asking if we mightn't join him and settling down with our lunch kit, I said, "You sure made a sweet run back there. You must know this river like the back of your hand."

"Why, no," our new friend said. "This is the first time I've ever been on it. I've been hearing for years about all the wonderful canoeing you have here in Maine, so I decided I'd come up this spring and give it a try."

"Where are you from?" George asked.

"Florida."

"Not much whitewater in Florida, is there?" I asked.

"No, I do most of my paddling in the Everglades."

"But you've obviously done some whitewater paddling," George said.

"No," the man said, "this is first time I've ever done any river paddling like this at all."

"Well," I said, "you seem to have a natural talent for it."

After we parted and the Floridian had disappeared around the next bend in the river, I expressed my outrage.

"Can you beat that? Here's a guy who's never seen a

rapid before in his life, and he runs them like an old pro! It's not fair!"

It wasn't, and it isn't, but there it is. It keeps happening to me all the time: The Song of Innocence, which somebody else sings, is sometimes far sweeter than the Song of At-Least-Some Experience, which I sing.

Perhaps the most devastating example was another Floridian, a young woman from Miami who knew nothing, absolutely nothing, about fishing. Before embarking on a Canadian canoe journey, she went to a local Miami tackle shop and asked the man behind the counter what she should use to catch trout and salmon and togue in Labrador.

The guy had never been north of Daytona Beach himself, but he didn't let that stop him. He sold Debbie a spinning rod and a big, gobby, goggle-eyed lure with a spoon face and a sequined azure body. I don't know what kind of saltwater creatures this thing was meant to attract, but no trout fisher would ever be caught dead within ten yards of it.

So when we get to the first fishable pool on the Rivière à

l'Eau Claire and we knowledgeable old hands are picking up our fly rods, Debbie tosses this obscenity out into the water, and on the first cast she says, "Oh, I've got something."

And she cranks her something in on what is probably about an eighteen-pound test line.

Something, she says. The something she has turns out to be a brook trout that people who have been fishing all their lives would walk through fire for. A trout that must go about five pounds, fat and sassy, just about as deep as it is long.

Dear God, I think, casting my bucktail out like a votive offering. Let me catch one that size and I'll forgive you for letting a total ignoramus with a spinning rod and a scaled-down rocket ship catch the one she caught.

I had a strike, a hefty one, and I thought my prayer was answered, but then I soon saw it was not a trout at all but just a modest-sized pike.

"Damn!" I said, "a pike."

And in the ten minutes it took me to get the thing in and off my line, Debbie had caught another monster brookie. There is no justice, I thought, and I had reason to think it several times more on that trip, because Debbie's Miami Special remained the hottest fish-getter of the next two weeks. She caught everything on it: trout, landlocked salmon, togue, and of course the pike that none of us were after but we couldn't avoid catching anyhow. The rest of us caught fish, but she caught more fish and bigger fish. It was awful. If she hadn't been such a great traveling companion, she might have been in danger of her life.

As it was, I sometimes sank so low that I considered asking if I could borrow her lure. But I'm happy to say that even in the face of that rank, cosmic injustice, my dumb fisherman's pride saw me through.

$\mathcal{M}$AP AND COMPASS

I DON'T KNOW any backcountry paddlers who aren't map freaks. No doubt there are some paddlers who are not, folks who slide their canoes only into local millponds or who are so addicted to whitewater and whitewater only that all they ever need do is drive to their favorite runs, their only map a road map.

But if your canoe is your magic carpet into unknown and—for you at least—hitherto unexplored territories, if your canoe is an extension of your arms and legs, a means of multiplying and husbanding your poor human powers so that your body can take you places it otherwise could not take you, if it is, indeed, an extension of your sensory equipment, a kind of antenna you use to feel your way into the world, then you will probably suffer from a dreamy, spacey, time-wasting addiction to maps that the unafflicted can behold only with pity.

I don't know how many winter evenings I've spent poring over maps of Maine, Quebec, Labrador, and New Brunswick when I could, perhaps with greater profit to mind and spirit, have been reading Proust or Tolstoy. A favorite starting point for these grand voyages of the imagination is a map I picked up several years ago in the native-

crafts store in Goose Bay. It's a 1960 map of Labrador pub-lished by the Newfoundland Department of Mines and Resources. The scale is 1:1,013,076 or sixteen miles to one inch, and the sheet is large enough to reach from the Button Islands off the northern tip of Labrador almost to the St. Lawrence in the south, from Fort Chimo in the west to Battle Harbour in the east. It takes in the whole Quebec-Labrador peninsula and launches more trips in the mind than any mortal body would ever have lifetime enough to take. Who can see the Canairiktok River running into Snegamook Lake and then on to the sea and not want to go there? Who can trace the route from Menihek north to Attakamagen Lake and the Rivière De Pas and the George and on another 150 miles to Ungava Bay without wanting to pack up tomorrow and be off? Would it be possible to start in this watershed, worm through that chain of lakes, pole up this river, carry over into that watershed, and run down this river?

There are, of course, all sorts of things wrong with this, my Labrador pipe-dream map. It shows waterways only in the crudest outline and with no elevations at all. Do those blue lines represent navigable rivers or screaming torrents that no canoe could ever survive? Also, this map was made before Michikamau Lake and Lobstick Lake were absorbed into Smallwood Reservoir, which feeds the turbines at the Churchill Falls hydropower plant.

So to begin to know what might be conceivable, I have to pull out later editions of 1:250,000-scale maps, on which an inch represents four miles. Many a long and wild Canadian trip has been made using maps of this scale, but for any trip that becomes a reality, the cautious persnick is going to feel a lot happier with 1:50,000-scale maps. With 1.25 inches representing a mile, you can thread your way through labyrinthian islands and have a much better idea of just where the damn carry trail ought to be than you can on the smaller-scale maps, on which that same dense pack of tiny islands looks as muddled as a serving of calves' brains. True, for every one sheet of 1:250,000 you need, you'll carry six or seven sheets of the 1:50,000s. But for the added clarity it can bring, that extra pound or two of paper is worth its weight in gold, though sometimes it's not the detailed view but the overview you need, and if you're looking at the large-scale map only, you may not be able to see the lake for the islands. I remember emerging from a particularly complex Labrador archipelago completely disoriented and sitting there in my canoe, manipulating map and compass, trying to get my bearings in a bunch of amoeba-shaped marks on a piece of paper while everyone else in the party started paddling off merrily toward the southeast as if they knew just where they were going. And indeed they did because a glance at the 1:250,000 map had shown them that the islands were thinning out and that the outlet stream we were headed for lay at the end of an ever narrowing arm of the lake that ran southeast.

More often than not, however, it's the detail you want and can never get quite enough of, even from the largest scale map that is practical to carry. A map, after all, can tell you just so much. Blue equals water, and that's that. The contours of the surrounding terrain may give you a clue to how deep the water is, but then again maybe not. On Atikonak Lake, we went ashore in a small bay, looking for a hospitable spot to sit out a windy day that wouldn't let us venture into the main body of the lake. The water was about three inches deep, and as we poled our way into shore, each prod of the pole into the mucky bottom released noxious bubbles of marsh gas. And so that bay is noted on my map as Methane Bay.

Abandoning it, we rounded the next point and pulled into a sweet little cove where a sandy beach and some trees to windward made as comfortable a windbound camp as a body could hope for. If, however, we ventured out from the shelter of the trees onto the exposed sandy spit that extended a short way into the lake, the wind would nearly pick us up and toss us into the waves. We soon determined just where the critical point was and drew a line in the sand there. And so that point is noted on my map as Whoosh Line Point.

And so it is that all my maps are scribbled upon and all

my notebooks are full. And still I have nothing but the picked-over bones of the reality left when I get home. The most complete journal and the most exhaustive photographic record don't add all that much flesh to them either. Nor would a video camera running twenty-four hours a day. There is just no substitute for being there. Maps and books and films don't smell the methane, get chewed by bugs, feel the sun's power grow as it climbs into the sky, catch pike three feet long, and eat buckwheat pancakes.

Maps are abstractions. Green on the map equals woods, but the green doesn't tell you, in Maine, whether you'll be in a head-high tangle of fir blowdowns where it takes half an hour to go a hundred yards or whether you'll be walking under the emerald-green canopy of huge old hardwoods, their trunks rising like gray columns around you, a carpet of dead leaves under your feet and nary a stalk of underbrush to trip you up in this parklike terrain.

The map says there's a steep slope dropping down to a brook, but it doesn't tell you that the ravine is a slab of rock covered with moss, fifty yards of it, and the ridge above the ravine is a razorback of ledge with sheep laurel and caribou moss growing on it. The map tells you there's a small draw leading up into the hills, but it doesn't tell you about the string of abandoned beaver ponds reverting now to little terraced meadows where each berm of an ancient dam lifts you a few feet higher, just that much closer to the abode of the gods, and you feel as if you could be climbing the steps of an Aztec temple.

At best, a map is a poor, bloodless reduction of reality. With its arrows for true north and magnetic north and its 1,000-meter Universal Transverse Mercator grid and maybe another local grid or two to boot, it is the very image of the

83

reckoning, calculating faculty, of human *ratio*, overlaid on this fierce, sweet, green earth. We human beings have linear heads. We may be capable of following the meanderings of rivers and walking the valleys and curves and swellings of the earth, but we need the map's schematic picture, and we need at least that one constant straight line the compass needle gives us to refer back to. Without it, I can't thread my way between the amoebae and come out where I want to. I can't get from point A to point B in the woods because the foibles of my all-too-human brain keep drawing me downhill instead of up, keep pulling me into the line of least resistance in-stead of along the line I want to travel.

Ratio has its place. Without it, I might long ago have wound up a rack of bones somewhere in the bush. But the river and the mountain are Eros, not *ratio*, and when I give myself up to winter evening reveries, there's no doubt about where my love and loyalties lie. Map freaks don't dream of magnetic declination and mercator projection. They dream of the bend in the river, the smooth, green flank of the hill. They dream of being there.

$\mathcal{M}$ARLOW ON THE RIVER, OR THE DEPTH OF SURFACE

HEART OF DARKNESS is one of the great river yarns of all time. Granted, it's not a canoe story, but anybody who has poled, tracked, and portaged a boat upstream can extrapolate to Conrad's Congo.

Any story that's called *Heart of Darkness*, that recounts a journey into the Dark Continent, and that affords the kinds of glimpses this one does into the horrors of colonialism and of the corrupted human heart is bound to send literary critics into a feeding frenzy, like a flock of dabbling ducks, their heads underwater and their tails in the air.

I'm not saying there isn't something to be found underwater. Surely there is, but whether you're a canoeist or Conrad's Marlow chugging up the Congo in his collapsing tub of a river steamer, you learn that the best way to plumb the depths is to attend to the surface. A keen and experienced eye can tell by reading the surface what is hidden beneath it, and a profound reading of the river is one that does not miss a detail in what is transpiring on top.

Marlow is hardly a shallow figure, but he is—as Conrad reminds us early on, before Marlow's narration begins in earnest—a man who gives externals their due: "... to him the meaning of an episode was not inside like a kernel but outside, enveloping the tale which brought it out only as a glow brings out a haze, in the likeness of one of these misty halos that sometimes are made visible by the spectral illumination of moonshine."

Marlow does not always speak in those terms himself. Sometimes he, too, will use more conventional language in which truth and reality are hidden, subterranean, submarine, and the surface is the shell that hides them.

I had to keep guessing at the channel. I had to discern, mostly by inspiration, the signs of hidden banks; I watched for sunken stones; I was learning to clap my teeth smartly before my heart flew out, when I shaved by a fluke some infernal sly old snag that would have ripped the life out of the tin-pot steamboat and drowned all the pilgrims. . . . When you have to attend to things of that sort, to the mere incidents of the surface, the reality—the reality, I tell you—fades. The inner truth is hidden—luckily, luckily.

But at the same time, it is attending to the surface that is Marlow's salvation. He doesn't deny the existence of unplumbed depths (or heights), but it is not in them that his hold on reality is anchored. "I had to mess about with white lead and strips of woolen blanket helping to put bandages on those leaky steam pipes—I tell you. I had to watch the steering, and circumvent those snags, and get the tin-pot along by hook or by crook. There was surface-truth enough in these things to save a wiser man."

And when Marlow comes upon a tattered book left in a riverside hut, An Inquiry into some Points of Seamanship by a man named Towser or Towson, Master in his Majesty's Navy, what elicits Marlow's admiration for this study "into the breaking strain of ships' chains and tackle, and other such matters" is precisely its devotion to the surface truths. "Not a very enthralling book; but at the first glance you could see there a singleness of intention, an honest concern for the right way of going to work, which made these humble pages, thought out so many years ago, luminous with another than a professional light."

Conrad did not, I think, keep track of his images in any consistent, mathematical way. If he says in one passage that "truth" or "reality" is in fact hidden, below the surface, the kernel and not the shell, I take him at his word; but I take him just as much at his word when he speaks of the salvation of surface-truth, of the luminosity of humble pages concerned with the right way of going to work, of meaning aglow in misty halos illuminated by moonlight. His tale may chronicle a passage into darkness and the depths of the human heart, but the business of making that passage is conducted on the surface and in daylight; it is a business of

rivets, white lead, strips of woolen blankets, signs of hidden banks, sunken stones, and sly old snags that Marlow learns to anticipate "mostly by inspiration" but an inspiration born of attention to facts and surfaces, not to mysteries.

The facts and the mysteries, of course, are of a piece; the deepest depths have to have their surface. As Marlow says, reflecting with amazement on the restraint his cannibal crew showed in not eating their masters: "Restraint! I would just as soon have expected restraint from a hyena prowling amongst the corpses of a battlefield. But there was the fact facing me—the fact dazzling, to be seen, like the foam on the depths of the sea, like a ripple on an unfathomable enigma...."

Kurtz is lost, physically and morally, because he has lost touch with the surface. "There was nothing either above or below him, and I knew it," Marlow says. "He had kicked himself loose of the earth. Confound the man! He had kicked the very earth to pieces."

Kurtz—to understate the case grossly—would make a terrible companion on a canoe trip. I've traveled with his like, people full of eloquence, full of knowledge that can save the world, people who, in their own idiom, produced sentences much like Kurtz's: "By the simple exercise of our will we can exert a power for good practically unbounded." With their sovereign disregard for the surface of the river, for the signs of the weather, for where they were on the map, for keeping their matches and their clothes dry, they were floating disasters ready to happen, potential Kurtzes in search of their Congos. They were like the short, stout fellow Marlow encountered at the Central Station. When a fire broke out in a storage shed, Marlow reports, this man "came tearing down to the river, a tin pail in his hand, assured me that everybody was 'behaving splendidly, splendidly,' dipped

88

about a quart of water and tore back again. I noticed there was a hole in the bottom of his pail."

Marlow, on the other hand, can paddle in my boat any day. Even if he had never seen a canoe in his life before, he would make a strong partner. Attentive to surface detail, to gear and tackle and trim, he would not have a pail with a hole in the bottom, much less try to put out a fire with it. He might start a trip knowing nothing but would end it knowing a great deal indeed. He would know from the outset that, unfathomable as the water below his boat might be, what he had to attend to was right up on top. Only give the surface its due, he would know, and it will take you as deep as anyone has ever gone.

ᴍIDDAY SNOOZES

ON THE ST. CROIX, the river that forms the southern part of the border between Maine and New Brunswick, there's a beautiful campsite about two thirds of the way down the stretch between Vanceboro and Kellyland. The river makes a gentle S-curve, and the site is on the west bank of the river just where the lower half of the S begins its curve. A bit of ledge on the upstream end of this promontory acts like a natural wing dam, shooting the current out into river center and creating a large eddy pool that circulates quietly back along the bank in front of the campsite. Three red maples, mature but not immense trees, reach out over the pool, forming a green, shade canopy.

Dick Wolfenden and I arrived there about noon on an August day as exquisite as any paddler could hope for: temperature about eighty, a soft breeze out of the southwest turning up the leaves of the maples across the river, puffy clouds in a flawlessly blue sky. It was too early to camp but just the right time for a lunch break, and after we'd put away our fill of cheese, peanut butter, jam, and hardtack, Dick stretched out on the bank for a little postprandial relaxation while I started to work the eddy with my fly rod.

Finally realizing it would yield nothing, I climbed back up

the bank and sat for a while, watching the mesmerizing play of the river. The water was flat except for the riffle caused by the ledge, but in that smooth water, boils rose to the surface and raced on downstream. My eye was automatically drawn along with them, as it is to the rise of a fish in moving water. The boils seemed alive, or at least caused by something alive, and only if I fixed my eye on a stationary point across the river and kept the water in my peripheral vision could I convince myself that they were indeed generated by underwater rocks. No sooner did one take shape than it was instantly swept away, and then another one swirled up in its place only to rush away just as quickly as the first, as if some family of trolls were sitting underwater, burping and belching.

But delicious as the sights of this idyllic spot were—the maples, the little bogan across the river, the stand of pines near it, the sky, the clouds, the play of the leaves in the breeze, the curve and play of the river—the most enchanting thing about it was the sound, the lapping and gurgling of the water, not the rush and roar of a rapid but instead this gentle, soothing sound of moving water making its way around and over the low barrier of the ledge, then dissipating its energy, swirling, flattening out.

No wonder there was a campsite here. Of course the lay of the land was perfect, a high, dry, flat spot that would look like the Grand Hotel to anyone looking for a place to lay her head. But the river's music made it irresistible, and even though it was midday, I too soon found myself succumbing to the lullaby the river keeps singing at this spot night and day.

Invitations to midday siestas, however, are more often tactile than aural. They come via the skin, penetrate the muscle, and soak right into the bones. Bars and beaches, whether of sand or gravel, are natural places to pull up a boat and settle for lunch; and once you've settled on some sun-baked stone or sand to eat, it is just as natural to sprawl out after your meal and soak up as much of that heat through your hide as you can. If the medium is fine and amenable enough, you can just wriggle your lumps and bumps down into it and relax. If you're dealing with a cobble beach, you may need a life jacket for padding. But any way you do it, there's nothing quite like the cooked-through comfort you can enjoy with the sun beating down on your belly and the heat of the earth toasting you from below.

So comfortable was it on a little gravel-and-scrub-willow island on the Bonaventure that my three companions, Tom, Steve, and Jonathan quickly succumbed, and I was left the only one awake among three deep-breathing, occasionally snoring stiffs. I sat propped against a driftwood stump, watching an inchworm make its way around the edge of my notebook and two tiny, delicate moths perform a slow dance on my left hand. Their movements were so tentative that I

assumed I was watching the courtship of two extremely shy little moths, and I silently cheered them on.

"Come on, you know you like each other. Go for it. You only go around once, you know."

Shameless anthropomorphizing, I realize, but who but a heartless clod could sit where I was with the river slipping by his toes, his friends snoring peacefully by his side, a chestnut-sided warbler singing in the alders, the breeze brushing the tips of the black spruce—who could sit in such circumstances and not want to witness a moth marriage, a creature consummation?

The breaks we take on gravel bars or maple-bestudded points are, ostensibly, utilitarian. We stop to eat, to stretch our legs, to catch forty winks and recharge our batteries, but we also take them to see much of what we've come here to see, to hear what we've come to hear. Out on the water, we live in the large dimensions. Here on the gravel bar is where we make friends with the moth and the inchworm. Here, where we stretch out in the noonday sun and sweet torpor starts to overtake us, is where we truly have our ears to the ground and can best hear what the earth has to tell us.

ILE BAGGING

MILE BAGGING IS a bad habit that quantitatively minded Western Man is prone to get into. A mile bagger is on the water at daybreak, takes fifteen minutes out for lunch (or grabs a sandwich in the boat), and paddles till dark. By flashlight he then looks at his map and figures out how many miles he has bagged today and resolves to do better tomorrow, when he will be on the water *before* daybreak and will paddle until well after dark.

Mile bagging is not much fun, but even those who detest it may find themselves forced to it if they have been windbound for more days than they built into their schedule and have to push hard to catch a train at the other end.

You can be a mile bagger on foot as well as in a canoe, and it is only a small step from mile bagging to river and peak bagging. Some folks cut a notch in the handle of their six-shooters every time they "do" a new river. And then there is rapid bagging: How many whitewater stretches on how many rivers can you fit into a single day? Complex shuttles are set up. You run the "best" six miles of river A, whisk the boats out of the water, onto the car racks, and off to river B, where you run its "best" three miles. Then it's off again, with a quick stop at a mom-and-pop store to eat a few

Twinkies and drink a Coke before you hotdog down the best four miles of river C just before sunset.

$\mathcal{M}$ONET'S RIVERS

A RIVER IS like a piece of music. The score is basically the same every time, but everyone who plays it will play it a little differently, and no matter how many times you play it yourself, you'll play it a little differently each time. You'll be on or off; you'll pick a perfect route in every rapid, and each stroke will be crisp and clean and do just what you wanted it to do; or every ounce of river sense you ever thought you had will abandon you, and you won't be able to do anything right. And the river will be different every time, too. The water level may be way up or way down. The sun may be shining, or the rain may be pelting down so hard you'll have trouble deciding where the rain ends and the river begins.

River running is like music, too, in being a time art. The river and the music exist whether we happen to be playing them or not. But unless we run the river we can't experience it; we can't hear its music. And even as we paddle and play, the very things we are seeking slip away from us. When the piece or the trip is over, we have only poor snippets and tag ends of memories left.

For a photographer or painter a river trip is paradise and hell rolled into one. Every minute is tossing up a fresh flood of images that all demand to be recorded and captured, and no one mind except the mind of an omnipresent, omniscient deity could hold onto them all at once. Right above my desk is a photograph taken on Diver Brook Island on the Churchill River this past September. The time is late afternoon. The south bank of the river is black in shadow; the north bank is aglow with sunlight and the brilliant yellow of birch and poplar leaves in Indian summer. To the west, a rainbow streaks to earth like a multicolored comet against a backdrop of gray clouds, and the river, flowing smoothly here, mirrors the rainbow, the gold of the poplars, the deep black of the southerly shore. The sand on the tip of the island where we are camped shows not white but a gunmetal blue in the shadows.

This photograph is a source of great delight to me. It takes me back to that place and that evening, but it also makes me frantic to go back there again. It makes me want to know what this same scene on Diver Brook Island looked like an hour or two or four before we got there and what it looked like after we left. What does it look like now, in mid-January? What does it look like in the spring when the ice breaks up and charges down the Churchill with all the fury of some unending titanic train wreck?

Succumbing to the charms of any river tosses you on the horns of an impossible dilemma. Do you spend the rest of your life going back to that same river, to that same point on Diver Brook Island, knowing that no matter how many times you see it you will only have just begun to see it? Or do you move on from one river to another and from each bend in that river to the next bend, knowing that each river and each bend has its own personality and mystery?

Most of us deal with that dilemma by resorting to those

97

sloppy compromises so rife in human affairs: We keep exploring the new while fitting in, whenever we can, return trips to those rivers and places that have spoken most powerfully to us. Monet did not compromise. Devoted to an art that can capture only static moments in a constantly flowing world, he went back to the same bend on the Seine time and again. He was not a canoeman. His way of knowing a river was not to climb onto the flow and become part of it but to be in the same place next to it season after season, day after day, to capture—hour by hour and minute by minute—the shift from blaze of noon to evening shadow, from water hidden in morning mists to ice floes glinting in the winter sun. "Mornings on the Seine" is one of several series, like the famous "Haystacks" and "Rouen Cathedral" series, in which Monet rendered one subject over and over again under different conditions of light and weather, keeping several canvases in progress at once, moving on from one to another as the light changed.

What he wanted to do, as he said himself, was record his impressions of the natural world "in the face of the most fugitive effects." No wonder he painted rivers and river scenes so often. The river *is* a fugitive effect, always in constant flight from us, slipping through our fingers no matter how diligently we attend to it. The river in its constant flow and change is the image not only of our own lives but of everything alive. It makes the best kind of sense that any artist as devoted as Monet was to capturing nature on the wing would return again and again to the river.

Like Conrad's Marlow, he knew that the depths he sought could be found on the surface there if only he looked intently enough, and the surfaces he created are in themselves surfaces of great profundity. Stand back from a

Monet, and it is luminous image. Move in close to it, and it invites the eye into a realm of pure color and light, into the molecules and atoms of the painter's brushwork. Neither dimension is ever lost. Whenever I see one of Monet's river paintings, the shock of recognition is breathtaking: at once, the sweep of the Seine, the gorge of the Creuse, and, up close, the texture of what could be caribou moss or of rust-colored lichen on granite. In his static medium, Monet has rendered the river's fugitive effects with such precision that you can almost hear river music in what you see on his canvas.

$\mathcal{N}$ORTH WOODS STROKE

WITH EACH PASSING year, the list of things I wish I had learned and done earlier grows. Why didn't I meet and marry my wife when we were twenty-five instead of thirty-five? Why was I fifty years old before I learned the north woods stroke? The answer is, on the one hand, fate and that sort of thing. And, on the other, I'm a slow study. But better a fall aster than no aster at all.

Now that I think back on it, I must have come across a few references to something much like the north woods stroke long before I ever learned it, but it never really intruded into my consciousness until my neighbor George Dennison brought the subject up many years ago when we were paddling across Attean Pond on the first leg of a Moose River trip.

"You know," he said, "I read somewhere a while ago about a quick, short paddle stroke the Indians used to use. They held the paddle right on the gunwale, and after a while the knocking and rubbing of it would wear both the gunwale and the paddle down. You ever hear of that?"

"No," I answered, thinking quite honestly that I never had, "but why would they have used a stroke that destroyed paddles and gunwales?"

"I don't know," George said, "but there must have been a reason, or generation after generation of Indians wouldn't have paddled that way."

It was a cloudy, windstill afternoon in late May, the kind of day on which you make progress no matter how inefficiently you paddle, and we had plenty of time to cover the few miles to where we would camp at the west end of the pond. So we made some floundering stabs at teaching ourselves a technique that, as I would later learn, is still practiced in the Canadian North but is all but lost in this country. I suspect that early on in the settling of New England, some Puritan divine saw the Indians driving their canoes along with this graceful, efficient, and seemingly effortless stroke, and he thought to himself: "Gee, that looks easy and fun. We'll have to eradicate every last trace of it from human memory and develop a canoe stroke more in keeping with our American Dream, one that's wasteful, inefficient, and at least painful if not downright agonizing."

And so it was that we Americans became "arm paddlers." We reach as far forward with the paddle and drag it as far

101

back as we can. The power face of the paddle pushes down on the water at the beginning of the stroke and lifts up on it at the end. Energy that could be spent making the boat move forward goes into making it bob up and down, and because the relatively weak muscles of the arms rather than the large, powerful ones of the legs, back, and shoulders are the prime movers of this stroke, all but the endurance athlete will soon be thinking that the best part of any canoe trip is its end. Paddling at a slow pace you'll take some 10,000 strokes on a short day (30 strokes per minute times 60 minutes per hour times six hours equals 10,800) and perhaps half again as many more on a long, tough day. That's an awful lot of times to do something the hard way, and only a spiritual descendant of Jonathan Edwards could think there's some virtue in it.

But inefficient as arm paddling may be, George and I were happy to settle back into it after our abortive attempts at trying to figure out, with nothing but an abstract notion to go on, how that old Native American stroke worked. We pinned the paddle shaft onto the gunwale with one hand and flapped the blade furiously at the water, like a stunted oar, with the other. Only about one quarter of the blade reached the water, and because we didn't feather it on the recovery, we caught almost as much water on the return as we did on the power phase. Our canoe must have looked like an obese, tandem loon that couldn't get itself airborne.

After we had thrashed this way for a few minutes and gone backward at least one stroke for every two we went forward, I said, "George, this can't be right."

"We've got to get more of the paddle into the water," he said.

"I couldn't agree more."

We loosened up on the lower hand, which freed the paddle up some and let us dig more of it into the water, but because George still insisted that authenticity required hitting the rail with each stroke, we whacked not only the paddle but often our fingers onto the gunwale.

"I can see how this could be tough on equipment," I said.

"Not to mention knuckles," George allowed, sucking the blood off his hand. "But if we just knew how to do it right, it would really work."

Inept as our efforts had been, they had shown us there was something worth pursuing here, even if we lacked the practical know-how to apply it. The benefits of the stroke's speed and short power phase were obvious. Because the paddle remains vertical in the water during the brief application of power, no energy is lost to pushing down and pulling up, and the bobbing of the canoe is eliminated. The speed of the stroke lets the paddlers maintain the canoe's momentum because the interval between power phases is never long enough for the canoe to decelerate. This eliminates the energy-wasting pattern of surge forward and drop back that is inevitable with the long, arm stroke.

These, of course, are the lessons of physics that modern canoe racers have adapted to their purposes. They too take short, rapid strokes to maintain a constant hull speed. By using bent-shaft paddles, they too keep the paddle blade vertical in the water. And they too, like the north woods paddler, use the body's big muscle groups—the legs, back, stomach, and shoulders—to supply the power.

That last lesson was the one that George and I, who knew only arm paddling, were unable to grasp or to translate into a posture and technique that would let us execute fast, short strokes with our traditional beavertail paddles. Because we used only our arms, our flailing and flapping soon had us sweating, panting, and grateful to fall back into our old retrograde ways.

After that brief experiment, I promptly forgot about the north woods stroke, which at that point in my history still had no name, for a few more years. I did, however, during that interlude read in a *Canoe* magazine publication an article called "Traveling with Ease and Grace" by Garrett Conover. This is the most complete and cogent explanation in print of how to do the north woods stroke and why it works, but at the time I read it I didn't even realize this was the same stroke George and I had tried to conquer autodidactically some years before. As I said, I'm a slow study. Then, too, I no doubt failed to make the connection because Garrett's article said nothing about destroying paddles and gunwales or bloodying your knuckles, two features of the Dennison version that had been printed indelibly on my mind.

I wouldn't know the north woods stroke yet if the lead-footed fates hadn't finally brought me together with Garrett and Alexandra Conover. What I saw on our first trip together was a revelation. The scales fell from my eyes. So *this* was the north woods stroke; this is what those Indians had been doing for millennia; this is what George and I had tried to puzzle out years ago on Attean Pond.

The paddles rose and fell at what seemed to my then innocent eyes a dizzying tempo, but there was nothing jerky or frantic about the Conovers' movements. Their bodies rolled back and forth ever so slightly in an easy, fluid rhythm; the canoe glided across the water without a bob, a surge, or a twitch. Like the pumping of a hawk's wings, the short paddle strokes were obviously powerful but their cost in energy expended was low.

The secret of the stroke is that the lower hand on the paddle shaft functions as a nearly, but not entirely, stationary fulcrum while the power is supplied at the top grip by pushing forward with the whole weight of the body. The north woods stroke takes full advantage of the leverage potential of the paddle. The arm stroke forfeits that advantage because most of the power is applied by the lower hand close to the water level. Expressed in terms of a backyard analogy, the arm stroke is like shoveling gravel with a short-handled shovel. The north woods stroke is like prying a rock out of the ground with a long crowbar.

With the north woods stroke, you gain the mechanical advantage of an oar and oarlock arrangement; but, because the paddle shaft is *not* permanently pinned to the gunwale, you also retain the versatility of the paddle. When the flat-water turns into whitewater, your paddle is still very much a paddle, not an oar, ready as ever to perform the pries, draws, and braces you need in the foamy stuff.

When you row a rowboat, the tip of your oar describes a circle, the plane of which is perpendicular to the water. You drop the oar into the water, stroke, lift the oar out (feathered or not), recover, dip and stroke again. In the north woods stroke, the paddle describes a circle, too, but the plane is horizontal. You sit angled toward the side of the canoe you are paddling on, your on-side foot tucked in under the seat, your off-side leg extended out in front of you with the foot braced against the on-side of the canoe.

This posture leaves the knee of your on-side leg elevated slightly above the gunwale, and I found it helpful in learning the north woods stroke to think of that knee as my "oarlock." You don't pin your paddle shaft to your kneecap, but you should never let your on-side hand stray more than a few inches foreward or aft of it. If you do, you start backsliding into the pull-and-haul of the arm stroke.

Now, with your on-side hand either on or just slightly forward of your knee, hold the paddle across your body with the blade extending out from the gunwale like an oar. Drop the blade into the water by raising your off-side hand and slice the blade in toward the side of the canoe, starting to apply the power as you do. You should be leaning into your paddle with maximum power when the paddle is nearly perpendicular and as close to the centerline of the canoe as it can get. The power phase of the stroke will necessarily be short (extending only from about your knee to the back of your seat) because you *will not* let your on-side hand either reach forward or drop back from your knee.

If you're paddling bow, your work is over when the tip of your blade drops behind your butt. Back off on the power, feather your blade by rolling your top hand forward (thumb pointed down), slice back to the starting position, and repeat the cycle. The stern paddler will feather and recover in the same way, but before she begins her recovery, she will apply whatever minimal pry is needed to maintain direction. The return is almost entirely in the water, the paddle planing forward and naturally popping up out of the water as you turn it into position for the next plant. The circular pattern, all executed through that imaginary oarlock at your knee, is slice in, roll your weight forward into the paddle, feather and return; slice in, roll forward, etc. My friend George was right about keeping the paddle shaft nearly stationary at the gunwale, but I can recommend a knee rather than the rail for a leaning post.

Is the north woods stroke really significantly different from and much better than the J-stroke? Yes and yes. Because of its mechanical advantage and its utilization of the whole body, it is much less tiring than any stroke that depends primarily on arm power. Also, its steering component is subtler, creates less drag, and is therefore more efficient. Because tandem north woods paddlers paddle in unison (as do the bent-shaft racers who say "Hut!" and change sides every eight or ten strokes), less steering correction is needed, and what little is needed can be firmly yet delicately applied in one smooth motion as the paddle is rolled, feathered, and started back on its recovery.

Last question: If the north woods stroke represents such a quantum leap forward (actully, of course, a quantum leap backward into traditional Native American practice) why does it remain such a well-kept secret?

I don't really know, but one reason may be that the north woods stroke is a traveling stroke and only hard-core wilderness paddlers still travel the miles and miles and miles on flatwater that the Indians and voyageurs used to travel, though my own feeling is that this stroke is worth knowing even if you will never paddle more than half a mile. Another reason may be that the north woods stroke is quite difficult to learn and even more difficult to describe in such a way that anyone can learn it from the printed page. I have no illusions that my brief description above will succeed in that department. In his *Path of the Paddle*, probably the most thorough and detailed book there is on wilderness and whitewater paddling techniques, Bill Mason devotes three paragraphs to the Canadian or knifing J-stroke, which is the same as the north woods stroke, but also adds that "most people require personal instruction to master this stroke." I know I never could have learned it without Garrett and Alexandra's example and coaching. Unfortunately, there just aren't enough people around who know it and can pass it on to others.

If you don't know anyone who can teach you, find somebody. It's worth the trouble. The north woods stroke is not just an improvement, not just a little bit better, not just another quaint little gimmick to add to your paddling repertoire. It's more like the invention of the wheel. It is to arm paddling what Einstein is to Newton.

OXYMORON
AND OTHER MORONS

LAC PAS D'EAU (No-Water Lake) in Labrador would seem to be a living oxymoron if there ever was one. A lake with no water is not a lake, right? On its surface, Lac Pas d'Eau is a lake, a shimmering expanse of water about two miles wide and five miles long. But anywhere from two to six inches below the surface, it ceases to be a lake and becomes a large, wide flat of silt and sand. You can skim your boat across much of it with a pole, but the closer you get to the outlet, the shallower it gets, and sometimes you run so firmly aground that you have to climb out and slosh along, dragging and shoving your boat.

Then Lac Pas d'Eau pulls another fast one on you with its sinkholes, which remain invisible until you step into them and go in up to your armpits. Your buddies will find this uproariously funny when it happens to you, and you will find it equally funny when it happens to them. And by the time you reach the outlet of Lac Pas d'Eau, everybody in your crew will be drenched and laughing uncontrollably. By any objective standards, you're a bunch of forlorn, sodden lunatics in an infinite Slough of Despond. But as far as you're concerned, there is no happier spot on earth and your spirits have never been higher than here on these sandy shoals with the huge, brilliant Labrador sky overhead and the current of the outlet stream tugging at your heels.

What might appear to be objective physical misery coexisting with the greatest subjective glee constitutes an oxymoron too, and perhaps goes to show that it takes a moron to appreciate an oxymoron.

The glory of the bush, it seems to me, is often that way, leaping out at you with particular power at moments that would send any sane person running for the nearest motel. This past spring one of my most indomitable trail companions, Bill Geller, and I clawed our way in over roadless, trackless terrain to what most folks would probably call an undistinguished little backcountry pond about a quarter of a mile long. Much of the going had been through old cuttings where the new hardwood growth was as thick as I imagine bamboo groves to be. It was June, steamy hot and buggy, and when we settled down to eat lunch on a little knoll covered with Labrador tea and gray lichen, the black flies rose around us in clouds.

Again, by any rational standards, this was an awful place, and we should have been wretched and glum. But about halfway through our lunch and between mouthfuls of bread, peanut butter, and black flies, Bill got this bemused look on his face.

"I hate to say this," he said, "but I think this is fun."

He was right. It was. Why? Because, like all ponds, no matter how undistinguished, this one too was its own minor miracle. It offered no immense or overpowering vistas. Some boulders out in the middle and a perky little spruce knob rising over its northeast end were its only striking features. The elements were all familiar: the granite, the spruce and fir, the little marsh at the outlet end, our failure to catch any trout. But it was still a place like no other on earth. And if we had not gone there we never would have been there. Which, as explanations go, seems to me about as inanely logical or intelligently stupid as they come.

$\mathcal{P}$ADDLES

WOODEN ONES ARE best, not laminated ones, not bent-shaft ones, but classic wooden paddles hand-carved from rock maple and just as long as you are tall.

That, clearly, is a statement born of my own prejudices. Lots of people would disagree. They might argue for a high-tech whitewater job with a plastic blade, a fiberglass shaft, and a T-grip. They might want it nose-high or chin-high or even shorter. And their reasons for favoring their own pet paddles would be every bit as valid as mine.

A paddle is a very personal tool, one that fits the paddler and fits the kind of paddling that he or she does. Because most of my canoeing time is spent traveling in the north woods and because I use a north woods stroke to do that traveling, I like a north woods paddle, one with a rounded, not overly wide beavertail blade that slices in and out of the water effortlessly and with a long, flat grip you can grasp as easily from the side as from the top. The north woods paddle is as tall as you are so that when you're standing up to see better where you're going in a rapid, you can keep most of the paddle blade immersed without having to crouch down. The extra length also makes it easier to perform the basic north woods stroke.

112

Maple is a tough, hard wood and a heavy wood, but the paddle is carved and shaved slender enough to be light, and the shape gives it wonderful balance. A north woods paddle combines suppleness and strength. Under stress, the entire paddle bends and then springs back like a bow. Paddles with metal or fiberglass shafts are leaden and lifeless by comparison. And, of course, the hand-carved wooden paddle is beautiful. The grain of the wood, the grace of the design, and the work of human hands all combine to give the north woods paddle an elegance that not even the best synthetic paddles can match. The difference is apparent in people's reactions. When people see a beautiful wooden paddle, their eyes linger on it; they pick it up and turn it in their hands; and they say, "Now that's what I call a paddle." Or simply, "Wow!" I've never seen anybody respond to fiberglass and plastic like that. People are moved by this meeting of an exquisite natural material with the shaping eye and hand, by the respect for the wood—and so for the Creation—that is embodied in the carver's careful work. That's why a handcrafted wooden paddle represents about as high a technology as you can get: a functional, beautiful tool made by the end user from a renewable resource.

The respect that goes into making a paddle like this has to carry over into its use. Tough as a maple paddle is, it is not invulnerable. I make a point of never pushing off from shore with my wooden paddle and never shoving the canoe along with it in shallow water. And if I'm ever obliged to break those resolves momentarily, I turn the paddle upside

113

down and let the grip rather than the more delicate tip take the abrasion.

But try as I will, I still bung the blade against unseen rocks and unwittingly grind it into the sand. The varnish is soon worn off the tip; the edges are nicked; water penetrates into the wood. Two weeks of that, followed by a couple of days of drying sun and wind in the back of a pickup truck, and you've got a split paddle.

There are a few things you can do to lengthen the life of your gorgeous wooden paddles. One is to make canvas cases to use in transporting them. The battering a naked paddle suffers riding around in a pile of other gear or just dropped into a truck or trailer is appalling. When you come off the water, keep your paddles out of the sun and wind and rub some linseed oil into any wounds or bare spots where the varnish has been scraped off. Lacking linseed oil, use cooking oil or Crisco or whatever is left in the larder.

Another great favor you can do them is always to have a cheap, tough synthetic paddle with you to use whenever the going gets tough on wood: shallow water that's not quite shallow enough to make you reach for your pole but also not deep enough to keep you from scraping bottom occasionally, whitewater runs where you're bound to whack underwater rocks, and so on. If I'm going out for a day of rocky whitewater paddling, I leave my pretty wooden paddles at home.

Mohawk paddles are quite ideal as extras for the grunt work. They feel pretty clunky after you've been using a good wooden paddle, but with their ABS blades and grips and their aluminum shafts, they are are tough and durable, and you don't have to feel bad if you use one as an entrenching tool to level your tent site on a beach. Another great virtue they have is a very modest price.

$\mathcal{P}$EANUT BUTTER

I CAN'T IMAGINE setting off for a day's jaunt on a local creek or a month's expedition in the Far North without peanut butter. It may not be high on your doctor's list of favored foods, but on a canoe trip your top priority is not cholesterol reduction; it's caloric punch. Peanut butter—with some 2,550 calories per pound—scores higher than just about anything except straight oils and fats. There's nothing quite like it for keeping the furnace stoked. But not all peanut butter is created equal; not just any peanut butter will do.

A commercial of some years back claimed that "Picky people pick Peter Pan peanut butter." That is an egregious lie. Picky people don't pollute their packs with Peter Pan. Or with Skippy or any of those other homogenized, emulsified horrors that taste as if they had been blended with used engine oil and marshmallow fluff. Real peanut butter is made of peanuts and a dash of salt. That's it. But simple as that formula seems, not even all the peanut butters that adhere to it measure up. The stuff you'll find in most health-food stores, either in prepacked jars or ground for you on the spot, will do; but next to the *real* thing it is still, quite literally, a pale imitation. Pale because the skins are not left on the peanuts. The real McCoy is not a light tan color but a rich, dark brown. It is not smashed into a smooth pap but is left chunky. You can feel it as well as taste it: This is *peanut* butter.

Where do you get it? Mail order from Walnut Acres, Penns Creek, Pennsylvania. Roasted, chunky-style peanut butter, lightly salted. Available not only in one- and two-pound jars but also in four-, eight-, and forty-pound tins, just waiting for you to scoop it out in great peanutty gobs, pack it like ice cream into plastic containers, and set off for Manitoba.

$\mathcal{P}$ERSNICK

THIS IS THE noun from which the adjective "persnickety" is derived. Persnicks are thorough, deliberate people attentive to detail.

One of the surest signs of a riverine persnick is what may appear to be a compulsive need to coil rope. Canoe trips call for a lot of rope and cord—painters on the boats, lining ropes (usually fifty feet each) for bow and stern, a sack full of light rope and cord in varying lengths for lashing shelter poles together, stretching rain tarps, tying gear into your canoe. But with all that rope around, it is easy to hang yourself or tangle your feet in it. So when persnicks are through lining their boats down a drop, they carefully coil their ropes and stow them away. When they take down the rain tarp, they tie each guy cord into a neat little bundle and stuff it back into the sack. If they see a loose end of rope in a boat or around camp, they pounce on it, settle back on their haunches, and coil it up, smug and happy as a red squirrel working on a pinecone.

But there are other signs by which you can know them: Persnicks are meticulously kind to their own and everyone else's gear. They do not run canoes up onto gravel beaches. They do not toss duffel up onto the shore where sharp

117

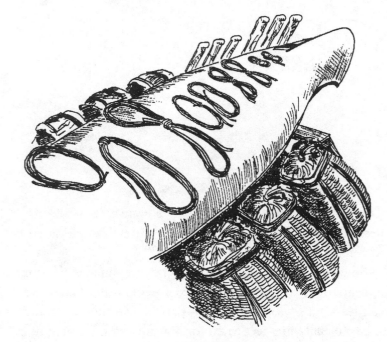

rocks can instantly poke holes in it or not so sharp ones can abrade it. They know that even the toughest gear wears out soon enough in the bush. Their axes are razor sharp and always sheathed when not in use. They always use a chopping block and never grind an axe into the ground. They tie up their boats at night so that rising water can't float them away. They set up a neat kitchen, wash up right away after every meal, stow food away safe from the rain. Water they have used for washing dishes, pots, pans, and themselves they toss into the woods well back from the shore. They don't leave their packs and wet socks and dirty underwear strewn around all over camp. They carry a bag for the small amount of unburnable trash they may accumulate. They keep their matches dry and have plenty of them. If they go into the bush to gather firewood, even during a monsoon, they come back with sound deadwood that will be tinder-dry inside when they split it open. The zippers on their tents work. Their raingear doesn't leak. They have plenty of extra wool in cold weather and a spare headnet in bug season. They know that there are three things essential to the success of a canoe journey: safety, safety, and safety.

Persnicks should not, however, be confused with mindless perfectionists or pedants. They are open to serendipity. They know that if their outfit is shipshape it needn't be bitterly Spartan. It can absorb the last-minute addition of a watermelon or two dozen ears of sweet corn in a cardboard carton. They also know that the kind of planning and caution you need to spend three weeks 200 miles north of Lake Temagaboogamie in the District of Keewatin is not required in everyday life. They have a sense of proportion. Persnicks are, in short, wonderful people to travel with. So when you put your canoe crews together, always pick persnicks.

$\mathcal{P}$OLING

ONE OF THE sweetest sights you'll ever see on a river is an old-time, north woods canoeman (I could just as well say an old-time, north woods canoewoman) driving his craft upstream with a setting pole. Standing forward of the stern seat, his canoe trimmed to keep the bow light, he plants his twelve-foot pole, climbs hand over hand up the length of it to drive the canoe forward, swings the pole up and out of the water, catches it at midpoint, plants it again, leans into it, and so it goes, the pole swinging easily and rhythmically like a pendulum—plant, push, retrieve, plant, push, retrieve.

By leaning slightly, by guiding the hull with the pressure of his feet, by planting the pole close to the boat or farther out to the side, the poler makes constant adjustments to the current. Always seeking out the path of least resistance, he hugs the inside shore of a bend in the river where the water is shallower and slower than on the outside. He ducks into the lee of upstream gravel bars and islands. He hops from eddy to eddy, relaxing in the slack water, driving hard across the power of the current to the shelter of the next eddy. He is a study in balance, river savvy, the husbanding of energy.

"Up the creek without a paddle" is an idiom that supposedly characterizes a bad situation. It doesn't seem so bad to

120

me. If you're up the creek, presumably your destination is down, and you've got the current on your side. Much worse is to be down the creek without a pole. Paddling a canoe upstream against all but the laziest currents is a killing job. Just as debilitating as the physical effort is the realization, brought home with every stroke, that paddling upstream is stupid. You're on an aquatic treadmill. You're going up the down escalator. The current is pushing your boat downstream; it's pushing your paddle downstream. You're at the mercy of a medium that's going one way when you want to go the other, and as the river picks up speed, you have to invest increasingly more energy just to stand still, a losing game all around.

Enter the setting pole. Poling upstream is far from effortless, but it has paddling beat hands down. Instead of trying to push against slippery, sliding, fluid stuff that is constantly running away from your paddle, you're in touch with terra firma again. Where before you had only fins and flippers, you now have legs and feet.

Provided you can reach the bottom with a pole, poling is the only rational way to move a canoe upstream under human power. But a pole is also better than a paddle for much downstream work, too. The rivers I frequent in Maine and the Canadian Maritimes are studded with shallow rapids that often have enough water in them to float a canoe but not enough to let you bite into with a paddle. The pole gives you positive control where the paddle can do nothing but scratch furiously at gravel or ledge while the water does what it wants with you. And as your affection for the pole grows, you find yourself using it in heavier and heavier water.

One great privilege the pole confers, whether you're going

121

upstream or down, is that it lets you stop in places no paddler can stop. The only way a paddler can really stop (in the
sense that the boat stops moving and the paddler stops working) is to pull into an eddy or go ashore. Otherwise, with a
paddle, the price of control is constant activity. And the
faster the river is moving, the more activity is required. You
can halt your forward motion by backpaddling, but if you
want to stay halted, you have to keep paddling; you're buck-
ing the aquatic escalator again.

But with a pole, provided the current isn't so strong that
it overpowers you, you can actually stop, lean on your staff,
take a breather, look things over. You can become a still,
contemplative point in a turning, frothing, roaring world. If
you've started out on a route that now proves to be a blind
alley, not to worry. Just take your time, see what your op-
tions are, and when you're rested up, ferry over to the left
about twenty yards where there's a nice open line through

this otherwise impassable rock garden. Or if you have to, push your way back upstream and pick a whole new route. With a pole you can buy a reprieve from the river's inexorable push toward the sea. I'm sure that if Archimedes had been a canoeman, he would have loved poling. It was he who said of the lever, "Give me a place to stand on, and I will move the earth." The canoe is the place to stand, the pole is the lever; and once you've gotten the hang of it, it opens so many possibilities to you that you feel as if you're pushing the earth around underneath your feet, putting it right where you want it.

None of this is to say that you can't screw up with a pole. Just about every disaster you can create with a paddle you can duplicate with a pole, and then some. That solid link the pole creates with Mother Earth is its great virtue, but that same link can be your undoing. Among the classic poling dumps is catching your pole in the rocks on the downstream side of the boat. The canoe then drifts sideways onto the pole, broaches, fills, dumps you in the drink, and breaks the pole off. Or, heading downstream, you jam your pole between some rocks. If you insist on trying to extricate it, you may stay with the pole while your boat continues on downriver. One of my fondest fantasies is to see a canoe drifting downstream with an oblivious passenger in the bow and a pole planted upright in midstream with a man clinging to it like a monkey on a stick.

The need for a pole may seem less apparent on lakes than on rivers, but lakes too have their share of rocky, muddy, and sandy shallows where, if you don't have a pole, you'll wind up using your paddle as if it were a pole, much to your own frustration and the grief of the paddle. By my informal survey, there are thirty-three bodies of water in

Maine alone called Mud Lake or Mud Pond, not to men-
tion all the equally shallow places that ought to be called
Rocky Cove, Three-Inch-Deep Thoroughfare, Beaver Dam
Boulevard, or Shoal Shore.

But if the the pole is such a wonderful device that no canoeist should be without one, why does canoeing literature
and, indeed, the whole canoeing world give it such short
shrift? The large-scale industrialization of the north woods
and of canoes and canoeing that followed on the heels of
World War II is the great culprit. The bulldozers that had
built roads and air strips in the jungles of the South Pacific
came back to Maine and started building woods roads here.
Logs and pulpwood would no longer be cut only in the winter and floated out to the mills on the spring freshet. They
would be cut year round and hauled out by huge trucks on
a network of logging roads that now, in Maine, total 11,000
to 12,000 miles. Roads now penetrate into practically every
corner of the state's supposedly wild lands, and hundreds of
miles of new logging roads are built each year. When the
waterways were the major transportation routes, people had
to travel both ways on them, not just downstream. But once
you could drive just about anywhere, there was no need to
push a canoe upriver anymore. River canoeing became, and
has pretty much remained, a downstream game. And if anyone did want to go upstream, the outboard motor, which
also came into its own after the war, was the tool most people reached for on waterways big enough and deep enough
to accomodate motors. On smaller, shallower ones, upstream travel was a thing of the past.

When I applied for my first guide's license in 1956, the
form I filled out still paid lip service to the Maine guide tradition of poling and asked me if I knew how. To my relief,

nobody asked me to demonstrate. I would have made a dismal showing, and so, I suspect, would most of the guides I knew. Poles were just not standard equipment in anybody's boats or hands at that time, certainly not in western Maine at any rate.

Things in the world at large had not changed significantly twenty-five years later, though in my own little world I had taught myself to be a much better poler than I was in 1956. At a canoe show in Orono in the early 1980s, Nick Albans, who was a member of the commission that tested applicants for guides' licenses at the time, suggested to me that I—or someone, anyone—should offer some clinics in poling because none of the candidates he was testing had even heard of canoe poles, much less used them. "If these guys had a sick or injured client and their outboard motors quit on them, they'd be helpless," Nick complained.

Happily, though, poling and its practitioners did not die out altogether in those bleak years. Old-time guides like Mick Fahey and Myron Smart were passing the art on to younger folks who were eager to learn it and rid themselves of the downstream-only blinders that most of the canoeing world seemed to have put on. And at the same time, a high-tech, racing school of poling was developing, launched by the Beletz brothers of Missouri, who first started using aluminum poles to pole unloaded canoes as fast as possible on combined up- and downstream runs and through slalom courses.

The Missouri School was soon followed and quickly surpassed, both in equipment and performance, by the Connecticut School, the leading light of which was a tall, young YMCA director from Niantic named Harry Rock. Using a light Kevlar Explorer canoe built by Mad River and a twelve-foot aircraft aluminum pole and training intensively both on the river and in the weight room, Harry developed into a powerful and skillful poler who has won the American Canoe Association poling championships in both wildwater and slalom racing for the past nine years. Presently chairman of the ACA poling committee, Harry is the undisputed guru of poling racers.

The racing style is to traditional north woods poling what, say, skating on cross-country skis is to traditional cross-country skiing. In competitive poling, there is a premium not only on speed but also on negotiating increasingly difficult runs. A poler who has developed some confidence in Class II water will start tackling Class III. In traditional poling, as in genuinely *cross-country* skiing, the idea is to travel in the woods—on water or snow—with maximum grace, comfort, and pleasure but minimal risk. If the water or the hill gets too steep for your strength or skill, you may choose to take to your feet. A spill that is just part of the fun with an empty boat at a poling clinic is an extremely unwelcome inconvenience, if not worse, for a backcountry canoeist with a boat full of gear.

But despite these differences in focus and some differences in technique, backcountry and competitive polers have more in common than not. The great benefits they all share are flexibility and freedom. If you're sick of mowing the grass on a Saturday afternoon and want to get out on the river for a few hours, you just pick up your boat and pole and go. You don't have to make arrangements with anybody else; you don't have to leave one car at the take-out before you drive another car to the put-in. You just go to the river, mosey upstream for a while, maybe explore up a little tributary as far as it will let you go, watch mother merganser and her brood swim all in a row along the shore, dive off that big rock ledge if you need to cool off. Then, when it's time to go home, you spin your boat around and let the current and whatever energy you want to invest take you back downstream again. It's this independence, this ability to take solo, spur-of-the-moment minitrips on the river, that nourishes a contemplative streak in almost all polers; and so it is that the mammoth-shouldered athlete who can power his boat up some daunting drops will also love to spend an afternoon out on the water just quietly messing around.

So essential is the pole to my canoeing life that it would seem logical to me for all beginning canoeists to start poling before they learn paddling. A pole was surely the first means of propelling watercraft, just as a floating log was probably the first canoe. I have no idea how many millennia went by before somebody decided that, when the water got too deep to reach the bottom with a pole, it would be smart to shorten the pole up and flatten one end of it into a blade. The paddle was a wonderful invention I would never want to be without, but it should not be allowed to totally eclipse the pole. Fingers, as any child will remind you, were invented before forks.

POST-PADDLING ROCK-A-BABY SYNDROME

I'VE ALWAYS ASSUMED this phenomenon has something to do with the equilibrium juice that sloshes around in your inner ear. But the few medical folks I've asked about it couldn't explain exactly what the mechanism is or why it works at some times and not at others. Miracle and mystery still hold sway.

It comes over me after a long day of lake paddling when the wave action has been just right, not a ripple, not a chop, not big rollers that keep you climbing and diving but just a gentle, easy rise and fall, a rhythm like a sleeper's breathing. Huge Canadian lakes are particularly conducive to it, those vast expanses of blue water separated from the blue of the sky only by a thin line of green in the distance. Here, water is the dominant element, and after you have been rocked and cradled in its soft pulsing for six or seven hours, fifteen or twenty miles, you carry that rhythm ashore with you. The land lifts and settles under your feet, and if you lie back on a sun-warmed ledge and close your eyes, you feel that same pulse and breath in the rock, on so-called terra firma.

If this unexpected treat comes your way, take some time off to enjoy it. It passes all too soon, and the camp chores can wait.

QNS AND L

WHILE GOVERNMENTS MAY be responsible for some of the more ominous sets of initials in our recent history—FBI and KGB and HUAC and SDI and PAC—railroads are responsible for some of the most romantic. The romance does not reside in the mere letters themselves but in what we know they stand for—places we haven't been but to which we'd like to go. The CP, for instance, the Canadian Pacific. Who wouldn't want to get on in St. John, New Brunswick, and ride through to Vancouver, with layovers, of course, in Winnipeg and Moose Jaw, in Medicine Hat and Calgary? I grew up alongside a dinky little commuter line in suburban New Jersey, the DL and W, the Delaware, Lackawanna, and Western. I knew it didn't do much besides carry a lot of actuaries back and forth from Hoboken every day, but it had a ring to it anyhow, some nice alliteration, some nice assonance. Lackawanna rhymes with Susquehanna, which is one big, long, sweet, swooping river; and "Western" promised even more, much more, no doubt, than the little DL and W could actually deliver.

The QNS and L—the Quebec North Shore and Labrador Railway—promises plenty and delivers every bit of it. Unless your pockets are lined with gold and you can hire bush

129

planes, the QNS and L will be your only means of access to
the Quebec-Labrador interior. Completed in 1954 to ship
iron ore from the mines at Schefferville, Quebec, to the port
of Sept Îles on the north shore of the St. Lawrence, the railway runs 360 miles almost due north, climbing steadily up
the Moisie, Nipissis, and Wacouno river valleys onto the
Labrador plateau. Iron ore is the railway's reason for being,
but once a week a passenger and freight train goes north to
Schefferville and comes back down south the next day. The
number of lakes, rivers, and streams the train encounters in
its 360-mile run is huge, and the number of canoe journeys

that can be launched from trackside must approach infinity, for the waterways of the Quebec-Labrador tableland are truly labyrinthian.

Time, it is said, waits for no one; but the QNS and L will wait for anybody. It will also stop for anybody—anywhere and anytime. The QNS and L is a railway run by the people and for the people. Unlike Swiss trains, which leave precisely at 9:23 if the schedule says 9:23, the QNS and L leaves when it feels like it. About the only thing one can reliably say about its schedule is that it will go north on Thursday and come south on Friday.

It is supposed to leave Sept Îles at 8:00 A.M. Sometimes it does, and if it does, everyone on board looks a bit startled. The normal routine is for 8:00 A.M. to come and go with a long line of people still at the ticket counter and extending back out the door onto the sidewalk. And for every person waiting in line, there are four to eight more out on the platform, milling around in the parking lot, smoking, talking, waiting. No one is worried, no one is in a hurry.

Standing in the crowd outside the ticket office, you realize that one thing the QNS and L does have in common with Swiss trains is cosmopolitanism, though the languages spoken here are not French, German, and Italian but French, English, and Montagnais. In the pretrain days, the Montagnais Indians used to make their way north to their winter trapping grounds on the Height of Land by canoeing upstream on the Moisie, a river that is challenging enough to run downstream. Contemplating feats like that should teach even the most competent modern-day wilderness paddlers humility. As Garrett Conover once remarked, "The traveling the Grand River trappers and the native peoples of Quebec and Labrador did routinely as part of their everyday

131

lives makes the kinds of trips we take nowadays look like walks to the corner drugstore."

The Montagnais knew how to navigate the rivers, and they know how to navigate the QNS and L, too. They climb aboard with pillows and blankets, make their beds on the seats, and, with hats pulled over their eyes, settle in for a little snooze. The air fills with cigarette smoke and music from boom boxes and cassette recorders. Every car has a couple of masonite boards in it that four cardplayers can lay on their knees and use for a table. Mothers nurse their infants; kids of all ages start scampering from car to car like squirrels and chipmunks, clambering around and over and under empty seats, running toy cars and tractors up and down the aisles, snacking on potato chips and Coke.

This is no commuter train. Nobody is in rapid transit. Most passengers on the QNS and L are in for a ten- or

twelve-hour ride. Life is not held in abeyance here, not put down when you board the train and resumed again when you get off. Life goes on. People, eat, sleep, pee, talk, play, go for walks up and down the aisles, stand on the platforms between the cars, watch the spectacular river gorges slip by, then the black spruce and caribou moss and string bogs of the taiga. Phil, a tall, powerful, gray-haired trainman from Newfoundland, comes through the cars periodically, picking up squashed coffee cups and candy wrappers, stopping to gab and joke and tell us about his brief career as a Newfoundland fisherman.

"When I was fifteen," he says, "my father came home one night and said to me, 'You are going fishing tomorrow.' So I went fishing. Up at five in the morning, seasick all day, and I seldom got to bed before eleven at night. God, it was awful, hauling those nets in the freezing cold and wet and heaving your insides out at the same time. So if you wonder how I wound up a trainman in Labrador, that's how."

Once the train is underway, it stops a lot. No one worries about that either. Some of the stops are built in. Once the twin diesel engines have managed to haul the nearly mile-long train up onto the plateau—a chore that makes the run north considerably slower than the return trip—the train stops at a big barracks where a maintenance crew lives and where the train crew goes in for lunch. And at Ross Bay Junction, the train runs off onto a siding where cars traveling west on a rail spur to Wabush and Labrador City are unhitched. After an hour's backing up, bumping around, pulling forward, backing and bumping some more, the train will roll out onto the main line and head north again.

Those are stops you can reckon with. At the unpredictable ones, the train grinds to a halt at some unlikely milepost in the

133

bush, and an Indian family piles off lugging armfuls of sleeping bags, outboard motors, fishing rods, cartons of groceries. Or the train simply stops and no one gets off. After fifteen or twenty minutes, someone will ask, "Why have we stopped?"

No one will know until a trainman happens through and says the track crew five miles ahead was supposed to have finished a repair job by now, but they ran into some snags. They'll need another half hour or so to wrap up.

Preferring to have the track crew, not the train, run into some snags, we passengers settle back in our seats for another snooze or head for the canteen car for the day's twelfth cup of tea or seventh hamburger.

Or the train may hit a moose. Adult moose are hefty beasts, typically weighing in at about half a ton, but you'd still think a mile-long train wouldn't register the slightest tremor from an encounter with one. Not so. The jolt sends anyone walking in the aisles stumbling forward or backward, flailing for a handhold on the nearest seats.

The train stops again. It did not hit the animal head on and kill it on the spot. The moose was trotting on the tracks in the same direction the train was traveling, and the engine came up on it from behind, knocking it into the ditch. A rifle is produced from the baggage car, and the wounded animal dispatched. The incident unleashes fierce debate on the train because some passengers want to haul the animal aboard, butcher it, and so prevent the meat from going to waste. But they are overruled by the train crewmen who seem reluctant to turn the baggage car into an impromptu butcher shop, and the train pulls away, leaving the carcass for the wolves and ravens.

Much of the talk about the dead moose is carried on by

five iron miners from Lab City. Their Newfoundlanders' dialect is characterized by rapid, lilting, rattling speech, by the use of the third person singular verb in the first person singular and plural, and the conclusion of most sentences with an interrogatory "Eh?" I find their talk utterly winning, but being somewhat hard-of-hearing, I also have trouble catching every word above the noise of the train. So a conversation overheard on the QNS and L comes to my ears like this:

"We comes down from Schefferville, eh?" the first guy says, "and there's this (rattle-rattle-mumble-rattle) caribou, eh? and before I could (mumble-mumble-rattle-rattle), helluva thing, eh?"

"Well, that's nothing, eh?" the second guy says. "Just last (rattle-rattle-chatter-mumble-rattle), eh? and so we goes up to Menihek, eh? and my snow machine, she bogs down, eh? and I puts the gas to 'er, eh? but the more I puts to 'er, the deeper she wallows, eh? and (rattle rattle rattle), eh?"

"Sure. Don't mind if I do, eh?" the first guy says, and the second guy hands him half a ham sandwich.

The train stops again at some place it ordinarily does not stop, and four new passenges join our car, two elderly Montagnais women accompanied by a young man and woman. The young people help their elders to a seat, help them out of their jackets, see they are comfortably settled for the rest of the trip. That solicitousness of the young and the middle-aged Indians for the elderly and for the children is, it seems to me, what sets the tone of life on the QNS and L. Amid the sprawl and mess that a lot of very un-Swiss people can generate in an eight- to twelve-hour day of traveling, there is an underlying sense of family feeling that communicates itself to just about everyone on the train, except, of

135

course, to the few arrogant, omnipresent, loudmouthed bozos who, wherever they are, remain impervious to anything but their own dreary yammering.

But the QNS and L is not just the train and the tracks. It is also all the whistle-stops along the way, and if you are leaving Labrador on the train, you will have the opportunity to spend several hours at one of them. At Esker, the tote road from Churchill Falls meets the railway. This is where all the heavy equipment used to build the hydropower plant at Churchill Falls was shipped to. This is where the huge turbines rolled in on flatcars and were then trucked in another 115 miles to the plant. Esker remains a major junction today, the place where freight for Churchill Falls is unloaded and where passengers going to the Falls or traveling on by car to Goose Bay will disembark.

Esker does not make a good first impression. A couple of run-down mobile homes pasted together are the dispatcher's quarters and office. There are the usual big fuel tanks, rail sidings, and gargantuan bucket loaders with tires taller than I am. On the west side of the tracks is an extensive set of barracks, also composed of prefab mobile units stuck together. These once housed construction crews but are now abandoned and totally trashed—windows broken, doors hanging in the wind, interior walls kicked in, toilet fixtures tossed outside, BX cable torn out and strewn on the ground amidst egg cartons, ice-cream containers, rusting cans of Puritan Irish stew. The fiberglass batting that insulated the crawl spaces where the water and sewage lines run has been torn out and lies on all sides, faded a light pink from the sun and rain, looking like the innards of disembowled animals.

That simile comes easily to mind in the fall because the caribou hunters coming down Menihek Lake often gut their animals at Esker, and the pink paunches can be seen bobbing in the water at the jetty or tossed along the few hundred yards of road leading from the lake to the tracks. Esker is a place where industry and wilderness have met and where industry seems to have decided to concentrate its offal. Hunters and travelers have been camping on the perimeter of the railyard at Esker for decades now, and the area is strewn not only with the bones, feet, and antlers of caribou but also with plastic trash bags, lost boots and mittens, Styrofoam cups, the ubiquitous beer cans and bottles.

Esker is, in short, a mess. But, oddly enough, it is a mess that grows on you. Because it's a major crossroads it's a wonderfully sociable place. It's the place where, if you're going out, you'll meet somebody you know coming in. Or vice versa. Or maybe you'll meet the people you came in with going out again, too. You'll compare notes, see who actually made the trip they had planned, who got windbound halfway through and had to turn back to catch the train and get back to work in Hartford. And because it's wise to be at Esker the night before if you plan to catch the southbound train on Friday morning, you're there when the northbound train comes through on Thursday night. The cars from Churchill Falls begin to roll in around six in the evening to pick up friends and relatives. If the train is late, anyone waiting for it may have an hour or two or four or five to sip on a few beers, wander around the yard, chat with other beer drinkers and wanderers, and periodically check with the dispatcher to get the latest report on how late the train will be. Esker is the ideal place to get to know folks.

North-country people are, by and large, hugely hospitable and gregarious. Give them time to kill, and they'll kill it talking.

The southbound train is supposed to reach Esker at about 10:00 A.M., so you break camp in good time in the morning and get all your gear trackside. But if word has it that the train still hasn't left Schefferville, you keep a hobo fire going, keep some water hot, keep a lunch pack handy, invite your neighboring hobos over for a snack and a cup of coffee.

The next report, at eleven, says the train still hasn't left Schefferville, so you break out a couple of envelopes of Knorr soup, the last dregs of peanut butter, a pack of Ryvita crackers, and get as serious as you can about lunch. You wander down to the jetty where the wind is raising a fierce chop on Menihek Lake and rejoice that you are not out there in a canoe. You wander the caribou-moss flats, kicking cans and studying expended shotgun shells, come back to the fire, rummage for the makings of hot chocolate, hunker your shoulders up against the wind.

On the lee side of the trashed barracks, you find some immense metal washers about three or four inches across. You drive a couple of old railroad spikes into the ground about thirty feet apart and use the washers as mini-horseshoes. Heated contests follow, complete with scorecards scratched in the gritty, cindery dirt.

It's three o'clock, the train has still not come, and everyone has played enough horseshoes. You find a sheltered, sun-soaked nook out of the wind and stretch out for a little nap. You get up, make the last round of tea and coffee, put out the fire, rinse out the pot and cups, stow everything away. The train, word has it, is due in about five.

At quarter of six, you can hear the humming of the big

diesels, and when the train finally rolls in, everyone leaps into action, carting canoes and duffel to the waiting hands of the baggage-car crew. But despite the haste the crewmen have urged upon you, the train does not leave once you're aboard. It has some freight cars to drop off at Esker and a few more to pick up. It advances on one track, switches are thrown, it retreats on another. You get to see your hobo campsite drop away behind you, then reappear as the train takes you back to where you started from. You sit for another fifteen minutes; the train rolls backwards toward Schefferville, stops, sits, jolts forward again.

You have time to grow downright nostalgic about Esker, to remember what fun it was playing horseshoes with outsized washers, to look across the battered roofs of the barracks into the huge Labrador sky stratified now with layers of gray-blue cloud backlit—and sometimes pierced—by a brilliant wash of afternoon light.

"Dear God," you think, "what a lovely pigpen this Esker is. What a gorgeous garbage dump, what a joy and delight and privilege to have camped here among the caribou feet and Oscar Mayer baloney wrappers."

Finally, the great steel caterpillar is composed, all its segments hung on. It sets off on its long crawl to the St. Lawrence, and I, for one, leave Esker behind with more regret than ever I left London or Paris, Vienna or Rome.

The final act is played in Sept Îles. After ten or eleven hours the train runs into its home port, and whether arrival time is eight in the evening or five in the morning, the snoozing, smoking, gabbing, card-playing, snacking population of this soporific train leaps into action the instant the wheels stop turning. People pour out of the passenger cars; a babel of tongues fills the platform; the baggage car doors slide open and begin spewing ATVs, dirt bikes, aluminum boats, canoes, packs, paddles, rifle cases, plastic garbage bags full of clothes and sleeping bags, Coleman coolers, bow saws, axes. Down on the platform, upraised arms clamor and jostle silently like the beaks of baby birds waiting to be fed. People move at a frantic, jerky, silent-movie pace, shuttling their gear out to the cars and pickup trucks parked just outside the platform gate, then scurrying back for another load.

It is early October, and the most prevalent containers are cardboard cartons sealed shut with plastic tape. The cartons are heavy, probably loaded with hunks of caribou meat, and their bearers do a shuffling trot with the boxes clutched in their arms, their backs and knees slightly bent. Their loads are so heavy that they want to reach their destinations as quickly as they can but too heavy to allow them to actually run with them.

Some hunters transport their caribou intact. A Chevrolet Blazer towing a trailer pulls up as close to one of the baggage-car doors as it can get, and four guys start hauling out whole animals. The side of the trailer is a couple of feet higher than the floor of the baggage car, and nobody knows quite where to stand. The four guys each take a foot and drag a huge caribou to the door but then are stumped. If they stay in the baggage car, they can get a good purchase on the gangly, ungainly animal with its long legs and a set of antlers the size of a porch rocking chair, but then they are all in each other's way if they try to lift the animal and drop it into the trailer. Finally, two men get into the trailer, and with some confusion, pushing, heaving, and hauling, they manage to tumble the dead beast into the trailer. The second caribou, just as large as the first, is even more problematic because the floor space in the trailer is now occupied by a tangle of hooves, legs, and antlers.

A small boy about five or six years old picks up a cooler that is clearly too heavy for him, staggers toward the gate with it, topples forward, and sprawls across the lid. Hardly missing a step, the man behind him swoops up the cooler and heads on out with it, the child trotting at his heels.

What appears to be chaos is not. Under the yellow lights of the station, mountains of gear and freight and hundreds of people move and are moved in not much more than half an hour. The platform is clearing already. We can drive our van and canoe trailer trainside to load our boats and gear. By the time we are ready to pull out, we are among the last few people left here. The big freight yard is empty. The parking lot is empty. The train itself is empty, too, looking now, in its domesticated stall, like any other unromantic, uninteresting train. But the next time we come back to it and it heads out of the station into the Moisie valley, it will once again be our friendly iron serpent, not a serpent that will get us booted out of paradise but one that will carry us into country as close to Eden as we will probably ever get.

$\mathcal{R}$ EAL FOOD

To SPEAK OF real food is to suggest that there is unreal food. There is, and it is spelled F-R-E-E-Z-E D-R-I-E-D. As I once heard a paddler observe after he had put away some pseudo-Stroganoffy mush in which the meat resembled croutons made of pressed sawdust: "You could *die* eating this stuff."

Real food, on the other hand, is spelled F-R-E-S-H F-I-S-H. One of the most compelling reasons for taking a canoe trip right after ice-out in Maine is to troll streamers for the lake trout that are still feeding on the surface in that frigid water. Lake trout should be broiled over a bed of coals. Properly supervised by the campfire chef, this somewhat oily fish discreetly dribbles its fatty juices into the coals, coaxing spurts of flame from them but never setting off a conflagration that can incinerate your meal. An optimal broil leaves the fish succulent, smoke-tinged, and so ineffably delicious that a theologian trying to prove to nonbelievers that the Word has indeed been made flesh could surely win his case by serving up some broiled lake trout.

In northern Canada, where the water stays cold enough right through the summer, a streamer trolled behind a canoe on a lake crossing may well yield this same treat in

July or August. And then there are the brook trout and the landlocked salmon, of which even the smaller specimens cannot possibly fit into a frying pan and so have to be slabbed into steaks for cooking. Nor should we forget the northern pike, those mottled green torpedoes long as your leg and with dentures that can take your hand off. Unfriendly as they may look and behave when you try to boat them and extract your lure from their crocodilian snouts, they make a superb fish chowder.

Unfortunately, however, even on the fishy waters of the Canadian North, you cannot rely on having fresh fish every day. And so, in addition to the peanut butter touted elsewhere in these pages, you need to take some other real food along.

In determining the kinds and amounts of food to take on a canoe journey, two simple principles apply.

You need plenty. Conventional nutritionist's wisdom has it that most folks burn about 4,000 calories a day on a canoe trip. Individual needs differ, of course, and energy consumption varies from day to day. A day of quickwater cruising when the river does much of the work will burn much less fuel than a day with several portages where you do all of the work.

The particulars of any given trip will dictate the form in which you deliver those calories. If you are planning a lazy, leisurely, cool-weather, flatwater trip that will last no more than a week, has few or no portages, and allows plenty of time each day for cooking, you can pile in a lot of heavy, bulky fresh foods and serve up *canard à l'orange*, asparagus right out of the garden, chocolate mousse for dessert, and a little fruit and Camembert to have with your espresso and cognac. (Also, if the trip is that cushy, you won't need 4,000 calories a day.)

143

Conversely, the longer, hotter, and more portage-ridden the trip, the lighter your foodstuffs should be, and the fewer perishables you can include. Frequent portages aren't the only reason for keeping your total outfit as light as possible. Heavily laden boats are sluggish and unresponsive and can make running even fairly easy whitewater difficult and risky. Also, on an extended trip that may call for long hours on the water, quick and easy preparation of a hearty evening meal is much more important than the eventual appearance of a perfect hollandaise sauce.

Most trips fall somewhere between the extremes of the lazy, fine-cuisine pig-out and the Spartan, food-as-fuel-only endurance test. You fine-tune your menus depending on which side of—and how far from—dead center any given trip happens to fall. Some things, however, remain constant, namely, breakfast and lunch, at which solid jolts of easily prepared carbohydrates and fats are the rule.

I don't know who invented granola, but he or she holds a permanent place in my personal canoeing hall of fame. The stuff is quick and tasty and sticks with you amazingly well. My own basic recipe is three cups rolled oats, one each of peanuts, sunflower seeds, and dried coconut. Stir in one-quarter cup of oil to coat ingredients, add one-quarter cup of honey, spread the whole works on a large, flat pan and bake at two hundred fifty degrees for an hour, stirring often. A cup of this granola adds up to about 666 calories. Toss in some raisins, add dry milk, stir in some water, and you've got a good start on your day's 4,000 calories.

If the day is raw and cold, cook up some oatmeal well laced with raisins and dried banana chips and any other dried fruit you feel like tossing in. Top it with brown sugar and milk, then see if there isn't a biscuit or two left over

from last night. If so, lather said biscuit or biscuits with butter and honey, and refill your coffee cup. Coffee is made in
a big pot. Bring the water to a boil, take the pot off the fire,
pour into the palm of your hand what is probably a huge,
rounded tablespoon's worth of coffee, dump the coffee into
the pot, a palmful per cup—more or less, depending on how
strong you like your coffee—plus one for the pot. Let it steep.
Jiggle and bounce the pot a bit to settle the grounds. Wait a
little longer, then pour. Snuggle the pot in close to the coals
to keep it hot.

The coffee will taste better, and you'll begin your day with
your eyes, ears, and spirit more open if you follow a little rit-
ual taught to me by the wisest of my river companions.
Make each handful of coffee an offering: "One for the
osprey. One for the moon still in the sky. One for the wind
at our backs. One for the wolf tracks on the sand."

Getting up early to make that first pot of coffee is one of

145

life's great treats. I love that first half hour or so of the day when the rest of the camp is still asleep and the only sounds are of your own feet moving quietly down to the river to fetch water, of your axe splitting out a little more kindling, of the wood snapping and crackling as the fire takes hold. And when the coffee is ready, you pour that first cup and settle back to sip it as you watch the sun sneak up over the horizon. It's the sensualist's perfect spiritual moment.

Then somebody else crawls out of a tent, goes down to the river to splash some cold water on her face, and comes back to declare this a good morning for a few rashers of bacon, which she proceeds to slice off that great slab of Canadian bacon you've got in the breakfast pack.

And the next voyageur thinks it would be fun to have some pancakes to go with that bacon, so he mixes up some batter and starts frying cakes in the other pan. And so it is that you ease into a pancake glut; and, between the cakes, bacon, butter, and maple syrup, you probably account for more than half of your day's calorie count before you even start breaking camp.

Lunch is always and invariably lunch, which is to say, peanut butter and bread, peanut butter and hardtack, peanut butter and jam, peanut butter and cheese, peanut butter and margarine, peanut butter and pepperoni, peanut butter and dried apricots, apples, or pears, and, for a little variety, peanut butter and peanuts. On short trips (eight days or less) when the packs can absorb some extra bulk, I take along homemade sourdough whole wheat bread and hardtack for lunch and bake only biscuits at suppertime. On longer trips, limited space demands that you take flour and bake the next day's lunch bread on the trail.

The native Labradorian trail bread is a quickbread called

146

a "flummy." A flummy is simplicity itself in terms of ingredients. The recipe as I got it from Horace Goudie, the most knowledgeable and revered of Labrador guides and possibly the world's champion riverside flummy-maker, calls for four cups of all-purpose flour, one soupspoon of baking powder, one teaspoon of salt, two cups of water, and three black flies (optional).

You mix the dry ingredients in a wide bowl, make a hollow, and pour the water in. Then, using a soupspoon, you carefully peel flour in from the sides, mixing it into the water. When the dough in the middle starts to get puffy, you start tucking flour in from the sides with your fingers and kneading it in with your fingertips.

"The whole secret is mixing," Horace says. "If you don't mix it right, it won't come out."

Now the dough is springy to the touch, and as it gets stiffer, you punch it with the first few joints of your fingers, and the closer it gets to being ready, the less flour you tuck in.

When the dough is stretchy, you put a little flour in the bottom of an aluminum pan (it has to be aluminum) and put the dough in with a hole in the middle to keep the center dry. And when you can feel heat coming up through the top of the cake, you turn it *only once*. Turn it more often, and you'll kill your flummy.

How long do you bake it? Until it's done.

"It's all feel," Horace says. "It's not a question of minutes. It's all feel."

The whole process is one of feel, a modest but rich display of practice, instinct, tradition. And the results are like no other bread I've ever tasted. A good flummy is light but not spongy, fluffy, or crumbly; it's firm-textured but not heavy. Like any real food that requires preparation, a flummy is a product of skill and care—care for the ingredients and the process, care for those who will share in it.

At supper, the carbohydrate flow continues unabated with rice, spaghetti, noodles, lentils, beans, soyburgers, and biscuits forming the base to which one adds whatever flavors and variations weight limits and the imagination allow. The secret of evening camp cookery is to make the spaghetti (or rice or noodles) you're having tonight not taste like the spaghetti (or rice or noodles) you had three nights ago. I can eat red spaghetti once on a trip, but the next time, no. I do most of my shopping for canoe trips in our local health-food store, where I can find whole wheat pasta and flour, brown rice, bulgur, millet, soy products, nuts, dried fruits, and the indispensible dried vegetables (onions, green peppers, parsley, leeks we dry at home). But the local grocery store supplies some essentials, too, like a Knorr dried pesto sauce, which requires only the addition of some oil. Or with a couple of eggs, some bacon, and grated Parmesan cheese, you can make spaghetti carbonara.

As you cook tonight's rice you toss in a palmful of every dried vegetable you've got, which makes as good a pilaf as I've eaten anywhere. And ten minutes or so before it's done, slice some kielbasa into it to add both flavor, protein, and calories.

And the next time rice comes around, add the dried vegetables and one of those small, unobtrusive cans of tuna or chicken to a white sauce or a Knorr mushroom soup made thick.

With some dehydrated vegetables, some fresh onions, and enough spices in your condiment bag, the possibilities for dolling up the daily grain or legume bash may not be unlimited, but they are vast.

The one department in which most canoe menus come

up short is salad. Chicory, endive, and romaine lettuce do not travel well in a hot pack, and the fresh vegetables that do travel well—carrots, potatoes, parsnips, turnips—are perfectly fine fellows in their own right, but what you want to offset all those grains and dried split peas and biscuits is not more pale, solid, underground starch but something green, crunchy, and leafy that has seen the sun.

Cabbage is the salad eater's salvation. It will put up with all kinds of weather and abuse, keep indefinitely, and, doled out judiciously, provide you with more side dishes of slaw than you would suspect one dense little ball could possibly manage. To add even more color and delight to your life, take along a red cabbage, too. Shred a bit of each, mix them together, toss with a little oil and vinegar. No matter how tasty your stew or goo may be, a little cabbage salad is always more than welcome. And if it should turn out that God is not a broiled lake trout after all, my next guess would be that she is a cabbage.

Needless to say, real food is cooked over a campfire. For broiling lake trout and the steaks or lamb chops I take along for the first night or two, I tie a small grate under the front seat of the canoe. For handling pots of stew, soup, spaghetti, or rice and for boiling the tea and coffee water and heating the pailfuls of dish- and rinsewater you want for any party of four or more, a cooking crane is the most efficient and aggravation-saving device a camp cook can use. Drive two poles about four feet long into the ground on opposite sides of the fire; then lash a horizontal pole about seven feet long across them. Suspend pots over the fire with light sash chain fitted with S-hooks at both ends. The chain and S-hooks make it easy to lower a pot down into the fire to bring it to a quick boil, then raise it again for simmering. Or if you want to take a pot off the heat but still keep it warm, you can just slide it away to either side of the fire.

This arrangement saves the cook the irritations of balancing pots on unstable piles of rocks and having to regulate heat by messing with the fire rather than moving the cooking vessels closer to it or farther away from it. And because irritation can ruin any recipe, it is important to keep all sources of annoyance away from the stew. Crucial, in other words, as nourishing, savory ingredients are to the production of real food, the human ingredients surrounding its preparation are just as crucial: ease, relaxation, lots of helping hands for the cook, comradeship, affection, liberal dashes of silly talk and laughter. With spices like that in your condiment bag, you may even be able to make freeze-dried Stroganoff taste like real food.

$\mathcal{R}$EENTRY BLUES

A DISMAL MOMENT comes on every canoe trip when you realize it's almost over. You pass under a bridge. You see a fishing camp alongside the river, then two fishing camps, then, around the next bend, three or four more. A power-line right-of-way crosses the river. The sky overhead is slashed by high-tension wires strung on the outstretched arms of pylons that look like crucifixes built with outsized Erector sets. Unless you have a rendezvous with an airplane that will spirit you away from some pristine shore, the last miles of any trip are inevitably laced through with the out-runners of civilization—logging roads alongside the river, the roar of machinery and trucks, powerboats, buildings.

It may take some wrenching to get away for an extended canoe trip, but once you're out there, it takes only about a day on the river before you've nearly forgotten there is any other world but this one you are in: the moving water, the curve of day from sunrise to sunset, the rhythms of making camp, working up firewood, cooking, eating, sleeping, breaking camp, moving on. The present is so engaging that the beginning of the trip is relegated in your mind to the distant past, and the end of it lies ahead in a future that does not yet impinge on now. But the sound of a helicopter whunk-whunking its way across the sky or the sight of a pickup truck on the riverbank, a pickup truck that could not be there unless there were a road that let it come there—sights and sounds like that rip you out of the clockless, calendarless life you've been living and remind you that there is indeed an end, and it is nigh.

At some point toward the end of a trip—and that point may come a full day or two before you actually pull your boat out of the river for good—the trip is over in your head. Even if you haven't physically crossed the threshold between out there and back here yet, your mind has, and you might as well not be out there anymore. At that point, you don't want to prolong the agony of the transition. Those last days or hours are a limbo, neither one thing nor the other, and so many things that are in themselves deeply satisfying on the trail now become strictly utilitarian. Camping in some place where you can already see a radar tower or the lights of a town is "camping" in a different mode. Your tent suddenly becomes a portable motel room, and though it makes perfectly good sense to use it that way, the ambience of tent-as-motel-room is very different from that of tent-as-tent.

Suddenly, whatever the sights or sounds or circumstances that have worked this sea change in you, you are back in your planning, working, anticipating, list-making mode. You are already thinking what you have to do first when you get home, then what you have to do second and third. You have already lost that sense of living wholly and fully in the present, a sense that is perhaps one of the greatest delights of wilderness travel, and you are already indulging in fretful mental sorties into the past and the future.

In Maine, where my own car is waiting for me at the take-out, I'll often push hard and long on the last day of a trip

and drive home in the middle of the night rather than make one last camp that is not really part of the journey I've been on but is instead just a reentry bivouac. It's like pulling adhesive tape off your skin. One quick yank is better than peeling the stuff off centimeter by centimeter, plucking each hair out one by one as you go. And the transition is easier in the dark than in the light of day. The darkness is a tunnel that takes you from one existence to another. You leave behind the sky overhead, the paddle in your hand, the water under your feet. You plunge into the tunnel and come out on the other side with a roof over your head, a chainsaw in your hands, and your wheels already spinning. The night drive back to so-called reality is a dream passage, even though you aren't asleep; and it smooths the psychic bumps of the return trip.

On Canadian trips, when the removal from normal routine is greater both in time and space, the letdown as the end of the trip looms into view is even more severe; but because the logistics of getting home are more complicated, there is no way you can rush through the transition. And

153

because you probably have a day or two layover in an unfamiliar place, there's the fun of exploring to soften the crash of reentering a man-made world. Then, too, even though you're melancholy about seeing this journey end, there's much to celebrate as well. After all, you've been out there. You're a company that's shared many a mile and many a campfire. You've got good reason to order a few drinks and propose a few toasts to the river and to yourselves.

So with all the regret that the end brings, there is also a sweetness that lingers with a keen intensity for days or even weeks. The memory of where you've been, of what you've seen and done, stays with you, and even as you sink into the depths of the reentry blues, you're also sailing high as a kite, savoring what is past and already daydreaming about where you'll go next time.

RIVER PIGS, TIN CANS, AND OTHER CRAFT

WHEN CANOE FOLK gather, talk will inevitably turn to canoes. Some of the talk can be strong. Canoe folk are, if anything, opinionated. They know what they know, and they know what they like. When Bob Davis, a well known wilderness paddler loyal to the wood-and-canvas canoe, was asked after one of his talks why he was so down on canoes made of ABS, Davis replied forthrightly: "I just don't like the fuckin' things."

Case closed.

If you look into the how-to literature of canoeing, searching for an answer to that question of all questions—"What is the perfect canoe?"—you'll come away well informed but none the wiser. Wisdom comes only with years of cranking on a paddle in different kinds of boats on different kinds of water. That way, you too can learn what you like and don't like, and you too will be able to speak with Bob Davis' brevity, clarity, and authority.

You will also learn that wisdom about the (near) perfect canoe is private, not universal. Your delight may well be the next paddler's horror, or vice versa. But none of that should discourage anybody from looking into the canoe books and *Canoe* magazine's annual buyers' guide to find out about all

155

the different materials canoes are made of these days and what influence different design features will have on how a boat behaves and what uses it is best suited for.

At the least, your reading will teach you a lot of lingo any paddler will want to know. You'll learn about sheer lines and water displacement and hard and soft chines and flared and straight sides and tumblehome; you'll learn about bow profiles and shallow-arched hulls and shallow vees and deep vees and flat bottoms and plumb stems and recurved stems and straight keel lines and shoe keels and no keels and rocker. You'll learn that hulls with flat bottoms, hard chines (sharp, nearly right angle curves where bottom and side meet), and tumblehome (curved sides rolling inward at the top) have great initial stability but next to no reserve (or secondary or final) stability. In other words, it takes some effort to start them tipping, but once they're on their way they'll snap over on you like a sprung rattrap. Conversely, shallow-arched or round hulls with soft chines (a gradual curve where bottom and side meet) and flared sides have much less initial stability and will feel "tippy" if you're used to the Staten Island Ferry; but, once rolled up on their rails, they display final stability and require some indiscretion from you or a good boost from wind or wave to send them on over.

The books will tell you many other basic things that are self-evident—even downright obvious—if you think about them a moment, but it's nice simply to learn and not have to repeat a lot of thinking that other folks have already done. You'll learn that a long, skinny canoe with a bow shaped like a narrow V (known as a "fine entry" in the parlance) will be fast because it slices through the water rather than bashing into it and piling it up in front of the boat.

Add a straight keel line that keeps this boat tracking in a straight line, and you have the essentials of a racing canoe.

On the other hand, if you take a canoe of that same length, make it broad in the beam, and carry that fullness far forward and aft, you'll have not a racer but a freighter. The bow will look like a wedge, not an axe. The canoe will be cheeky in the quarters, and its volume will be much greater than the racer's: great for carrying big loads, great for riding up on big waves that the racer would plunge into, but terrible for pushing through the water; in short, the quintessential river pig.

Because most paddlers neither race nor freight, most canoes are designed to fall somewhere between those extremes. Canoes for backcountry travel are asked to do just about everything—carry big loads, ride out heavy waves on lakes, be directionally stable in flatwater, maneuverable in

157

whitewater, and relatively easy and fast to paddle—so their designs often incorporate, with varying success, features from all over the map. They'll be long enough (17.5 to 18.5 feet) to remain fairly slim even with a beam of 34 to 36 inches. Entry lines are kept fine to ease paddling but then flare at the quarters to improve buoyancy and load-bearing capacity. There'll be some rocker (upward curve in the keel line) to let the boat turn and spin easily yet not so much that the canoe is impossible to hold on course on a breezy lake. And so on and on.

But once you've got yourself a wilderness tripper or maybe a somewhat shorter, lighter all-purpose, fool-around recreational canoe, you may well start thinking it's time to do a little flatwater racing or heavy-duty, solo whitewater paddling, and you'll be out looking at boats radically different in design. Or you may have seen another canoe that looks just a little more nearly perfect than the near perfect boat you bought the first time around. And so it is that canoe buffs acquire two and three and more canoes. Bill Stearns, a lifetime canoe addict, a canoe designer, and a founding father of the Penobscot Paddle and Chowder Society in Maine, quotes one Phil Schwind to the effect that canoes are like dogs. A poor man has one; a very poor man has several.

Design, of course, is not the only thing to think about. Materials are another. Before the end of World War II, nobody had to think about materials at all. Canoes were made of wood and canvas. There were still some birchbark boats around and some beautiful all-wood ones, but if you said "Canoe," chances are that anyone hearing you would picture a wood-and-canvas boat.

The industrial processes and materials developed during

World War II revolutionized canoe building and canoeing. Like most technological revolutions, this one, too, taken at first glance, may seem to have had nothing but beneficial effects. When Grumman retooled after the war and started stamping out canoe hulls instead of airplane fuselages, it made available at a fairly modest price a canoe that any duffer could clang and bang through a rapid without having to fear anything more than a few dents, a canoe that could be hauled over rocks and stumps and sluiced down snag-filled riverbanks with impunity, a canoe that could be hauled into a backcountry pond and left there in the puckerbrush year after year, winter and summer, without rotting or showing the slightest damage, a canoe that required zero maintenance, a canoe that could be wrapped around a rock, hauled off, and, if it had not been torn, could be literally stomped back into shape.

Now isn't all that a great gain over the poor old wood-and-canvas canoe? Isn't it a great gain for a canoe to be a durable, assembly-line, mass-market product that nobody has to worry much about instead of a handcrafted artifact that has taken many hours of highly skilled work to build and that, while far stronger and more durable than the industrial-canoe world would have us believe, cannot take the kind of abuse, major or minor, that an aluminum canoe can?

Well, maybe, in some shortsighted, short-term sense, if we assume that a tin can and a canoe should have identical qualities. But in the long haul, no. Take aesthetics. Aluminum canoes are just plain plug ugly, ugly to look at, ugly to listen to, ugly to touch. They're bulgy heaps of stamped sheet aluminum and rivets with all the grace of a bucket loader. No matter how gently you put a paddle down in them they say "Boing!" Their gunwales and decks cut into your hands. They're frying pans in hot weather and refrigerator trays in cold. Of all the canoe materials I have come to dislike, aluminum tops the list.

Fiberglass, Kevlar, and all related industrial fibers run a close second. While a good number of such canoes rival aluminum for ugliness, I have to allow that there are many canoes made of these materials that have elegant lines in a mod, functional, Bauhaus, Danish-contemporary-furniture sort of way. Innovative designers like to work with these materials because there are practically no limits to the shapes you can execute in them. High-quality boats of this type are made by laying a fiberglass or Kevlar cloth (or a combination of various high-tech fibers) into a mold, then impregnating the whole business with a resin that hardens. Kevlar is the stuff that bulletproof vests are made of, and it produces a light yet tough canoe. This is the technology that turns out featherweight racing canoes that you can see through. I can feel a detached admiration for the know-how that goes into these boats, but ultimately I find them unappealing and a little frightening too. With their aluminum thwarts and bucket seats and chemical hulls, they look a bit like the cockpit of a jet fighter, designed more for combat than for love of the world.

The cheapest and ugliest of fiberglass boats are produced by squirting a mix of glass fibers and resin into a mold. The interior of these boats looks something like the wrong side of a fiberglass bathtub-shower unit. Because there are no long fibers, there is no integrity or strength. A good whack on a rock and you've got a hole. Design? Take a scow, pinch both ends, and you've got it. A crummy fiberglass boat is a canoe designer's nightmare allowed to dry.

The one synthetic I have succumbed to is ABS (acrylonitrile-butadiene-styrene), which usually goes under the brand name of Royalex and is in fact a sandwich made up of vinyl, an ABS substrate, and ABS foam. Some fifteen years ago, I saw an Old Town Tripper going at a special sale price, and thinking it was time I stopped being a hopeless curmudgeon and got in step with human progress, I bought it. It has been a rugged, dependable boat that I have paddled, poled, portaged, and dragged for many a mile. Royalex is a quiet, warm material that is easy to live with. The hull is flexible and slippery, easing you over those rocks you should have missed but didn't. But because Royalex is thick stuff, it's impossible to mold into the sweetest and subtlest of shapes; and though the Tripper's lines are not the worst, it is no epitome of grace. While not an out-and-out river pig (though many paddlers consider it one), it is surely more a chunky work horse than an aristocratic Arabian.

But in the years I have used my Tripper, appreciated it for its good qualities, and come to think of it as an old friend, I have also come to feel more strongly than ever that in the Great Scheme of Things the only real canoes are wooden ones. Space-age materials and the canoes made from them are manufactured. Wooden canoes are crafted. Their production can be streamlined and rationalized, but they still remain products of loving human labor in which the beauty, strength, and handling qualities of the final product will depend on the builder's eye for wood and wood grain, his skill with tools, and his knowledge of his tradition. The wood-and-canvas canoe, which is the Yankee craftsman's adaptation of the Native American birchbark canoe, represents perhaps one of the noblest meetings of Native American and European cultures.

Then, too, a wooden boat is, in every sense of the word, organic. It belongs to the world of living things in a way that no metal or plastic craft can. Wood, even if it is not shaped into a boat at all, still floats. Aluminum and plastics do not float without assistance from built-in air chambers, nor do they grow in the woods where anyone can have them for the felling.

A wooden boat is responsive as only wood can be. Just as wooden skis connect the user more intimately with snow and terrain than plastic ones do, so a wooden boat under your feet is a living link with the water. The hull of a cedar canoe flexes, yields, and springs back like a tree swaying in the wind. It is incredibly resilient, but—also like the tree—it can be stressed beyond its limits and break. It has the limitations of a live being, and we have to treat it with the same respect. An ABS or polyethylene canoe can wrap around a rock and be popped back into its original shape afterwards, but we will always carry a cedar canoe rather than expose it even to the possibility of fatal abuse. A product of high human skills and of decades of natural growth, it is too precious to risk lightly.

But the distinction between industrial and organic watercraft is perhaps nowhere more obvious than after "death." An aluminum or synthetic boat that is damaged beyond repair is junk. You can't put it to any use, and you can't get rid of it either. A ruined or derelict wooden boat, on the other hand, will rot and go back to earth. A canoe forgotten in the woods, its back broken and its ribs splayed out, is reminiscent of a dead animal. It is a sad sight but not any more out of place than the skeleton of a winter-killed deer would be. It has its roots, in every sense, in the north woods, and it can sink back into the soil of those woods.

162

Given decent care, however, it will long outlast the toughest of us and can be passed down from generation to generation. Cracked planks and ribs and tattered canvas can always be replaced. Unless you reduce your wood-and-canvas boat to matchsticks, it can always be repaired.

More important than any of these practical considerations, though, are the emotional and aesthetic ones. There is simply no—I repeat, no—metal or synthetic boat that can begin to equal the beauty of a well-designed and -crafted wood-and-canvas canoe. And if canoeing is not about grace and beauty, what is it about? Also, instead of being a link to earth and water, the metal or synthetic boat insulates us from them. Every time I launch (or even see) a wood-and-canvas canoe the grain of the wood visible in the planking connects me with the forest; the visible skeleton, sweeping lines, and smooth skin remind me of some aquatic creature; the workmanship (if it is fine) creates a bond of respect and admiration with the craftsman or -woman, known or unknown to me, who built this boat.

A canoe should invite us to look at nature and our fellow humans with a loving eye. A fine wooden canoe, it seems to me, like any work of art, invites us to do just that but also to look a little deeper, a little closer, a little longer; and I can't help thinking that if we all paddled wood-and-canvas canoes, we would give much more thought to living well and gently in the world and much less to making first descents, breaking past records, and paddling bulletproof, aquatic Phantom jets down previously unpaddleable rivers.

$\mathcal{S}$AILING

I DON'T KNOW anything about it. The American Canoe Association has a Canoe Sailing division. Much attention has been given to rigging, leeboards, and whatnot for canoe sailing; and I'm sure that people who sail canoes are as happy to share their knowledge and are as great lunatics as people who paddle them.

My only experiences with trying to harness the wind have been on canoe trips when, with the wind at my stern, I've tried to rig tarps and canoe poles into usable sails. Lots of people seem to be able to do this with success and satisfaction. I'm not among them. I usually wind up with my improvised spinnaker flat in the water, the victim of an untoward gust. At which point I say the hell with this and just rejoice in the fact that I'm going the same way the wind is.

Wilderness paddlers who are really serious about getting a free ride lash poles across two or three canoes and make catamarans or trimarans, which are vastly more stable in wind and waves than a single canoe and so do not oblige you to throw your sail and rigging overboard to prevent capsizing. Maybe one of these days a huge body of water and a cooperative tail wind will induce me to get serious.

164

SEMI-WILDERNESS

WHEN YOU DON'T have the time or money to get into real wilderness, you make do with semi-wilderness. I don't know what the official designation of semi-wilderness is, or if there is such a definition. But I guess just about any large area in the lower forty-eight that does not have roads, houses, factories, and shopping malls on it would qualify.

Semi-wilderness, so defined, is a pretty loose and baggy concept, and one could quibble endlessly with it. What, for instance, are large state or national parks? Wilderness or semi-wilderness? I would call them semi-wilderness areas in which a conscious effort is made to preserve as much of wilderness as possible. They certainly look a lot better than vast patches of paper-company holdings, which also qualify as semi-wilderness under the original definition. It is hard to think of six hundred acres of clearcut as anything but a trashed landscape, and then one begins to calculate how many six-hundred-acre clearcuts a region can absorb before the integrity of the original ecosystem is so far gone that nothing of wilderness remains. At that point, terms like "semi-wilderness" or even "multiple-use forest" are no longer applicable, and it is time to call those lands "pulpwood plantations" and what grows on them not "trees" but toilet paper and newsprint on the stump.

Still, I don't knock semi-wilderness. If we took the idea seriously and really tried to manage our human activities in a way that left room for some wilderness in our midst we'd be way ahead. If many of my happiest moments have been spent in wilderness, many of the semi-happiest have been spent in semi-wilderness.

SEX

THE NEXT BEST thing to canoeing and fly casting for trout. Some people with confused priorities may disagree. I recall one fellow who had just run his first Class III rapid exclaiming, "Wow, that was almost as good as sex."

Anyway, one of the few times I think about sex only intermittently rather than constantly is when I'm canoeing or fishing. There is a time for everything, and when I'm on the water, I belong to it, body and soul.

That doesn't mean that sex has no place on a canoe trip or that a little human warmth isn't welcome at the end of the day. It's just that sex assumes much less importance among our preoccupations. If I may draw an analogy: You don't go on a canoe trip primarily to eat, either. But we all know how good food tastes after a day of paddling.

$\mathcal{S}$PIRITS

ALCOHOL IS FAR from essential to the smooth functioning of a canoe trip. If you forget it, you'll never miss it. The only truly essential beverage is water, and in canoe travel, there's never any lack of that.

But spirits are nice, and unless you're off on some Spartan undertaking where you expect to be portaging as much as you're paddling and need every square inch in your packs for those last twelve raisins that may save your life on the shores of Hudson Bay, some grog is one of those little luxuries that a canoe can easily carry, though you can't ask even a canoe to transport a fully stocked bar.

Beer and ale are out. A party of six on a week's trip, figuring on a modest two bottles per person per day, will need three and a half cases, a burden of a case and then some for each boat and a burden that no one without a twenty-foot aluminum freighter and an outboard motor would happily take on. Then there is the problem of keeping the stuff cold (it's hard to paddle a canoe that is dragging a six-pack behind it in a landing net), not to mention the huge, clanking trash bag. Flattened cans could ease that problem, but, even so, the mere idea of a trash bag full of squashed beer cans in a canoe appalls me. Multiply all this by a two-

168

or three-week trip, and you'll see that beer is definitely out.

Even if the practical difficulties it poses could be over-come, there is another and perhaps more important difficul-ty that could not: Beer violates decorum; it is a breach of style. Picture the perfect northern canoe camp on a pine point. The tents are set up; a pot of stew is simmering on the cooking crane; the biscuits are baking in the reflector oven. The sun is just dropping over the western horizon. The wind is dying, leaving only a gentle ripple on the sur-face of the water. The night sky promises to be a star-stud-ded, velvety black. There might even be a touch of frost, maybe even a show of northern lights.

Now I ask you: Does Bud or Coors Light or St. Pauli Girl or even Pilsner Urquell or Guinness Stout belong in this picture? It most certainly does not. Beer is for pubs, for hot summer afternoons after haying, for cookouts, for the terraces of monasteries in Bavaria where the monks really know how to make the stuff. Beer is not the beverage of canoe trails.

Wine is less of an insult to the ambience, and though it would never occur to me to take it along, I do not protest bitterly if someone pulls out a bottle and offers a dollop or two to go along with landlocked-salmon steaks. But wine suffers from the same practical disadvantages as beer: too much liquid and weight and packaging.

What a canoe trip wants is high-proof, high-spirited stuff in light, unbreakable containers. Among all the wonderful plastic bottles at L. L. Bean, you'll find some flat flasks with a screw-on jigger for a top. Beneath that is a much tighter, leakproof top. The larger of these flasks accomodates a fifth of Jack Daniel's or Seagram's V.O. or Rémy Martin very nicely. The point is quality, not quantity. Canoe travel is quite intoxicating enough. You don't need any chemical stimulation. I start feeling a little giddy the minute I climb into a car with a canoe on the roof. Once I'm on the river, the real high sets in; and I may not come back down again for days after the trip is over.

The strains and constraints of the cocktail party are left behind. No one needs anything to loosen the tongue, and the most appropriate time to pull out the flask is not before but after the evening meal when all the dishes are washed and all the camp chores done. The fire is dying down to coals; wool collars are turned up against the chill; and everyone is warm, well fed, hypnotized by the fire, enjoying the languor that follows a long day on the water.

"Anybody want a little brandy?" a voice from somewhere in the circle says.

When you splash just enough into your grannyware cup to cover the bottom of it, you're not a drinker, you're a communicant. The liquor is a benevolent firewater, a warmth that flows down your gullet and into your core. With this small, shared drink, you are celebrating the water that has carried you all day, possibly scared the hell out of you, and slaked your thirst; the fire in the sky that has warmed your back and lit your way, the fire on the ground in front of you that has cooked your food and is warming you now, the warmth of this human circle.

$\mathcal{S}$TOPPING

SOMETIMES I THINK stopping is what wilderness canoeing is all about. A paddler who doesn't know when he ought to stop or isn't able to stop when he has to is a menace to himself and everyone with him, and a paddler who never chooses to stop is so lacking in serendipity that he won't have much fun no matter where he is, so he might as well stay home and cover his miles on the commuter train.

I exaggerate, of course. A trip plagued by too many enforced stops or slowdowns—to wait out winds or to slog your way through endless bogs at a quarter of a mile per hour—can begin to gnaw away at morale, too; and after a day or two like that even the most pause-prone paddler will want to get *on* with it, to crank on her paddle from morning till night, and be able to say at supper that evening, "Terrific! We did twenty-six miles today."

Clearly there is some ideal balance between moving on and sitting still, and if I were given to reflections on the yin and the yang, on thesis, antithesis, and synthesis, I would have some spiffy, universally valid moral to promulgate here. As it is, all I can offer is that haste, either deliberately chosen or slithered into, is by far the more common enemy of safe, comfortable, and enjoyable canoe journeys than are slowing down and stopping.

172

If you're a downriver racer, the measure of your skill and prowess is how fast you can get from point A upstream to point B downstream. Fast runs call not only for physical power and endurance and squeezing the maximum efficiency out of every paddle stroke; they also call for river savvy—picking the currents that will speed you on your way, avoiding the ones that will work against you, keeping out of the waves that will, if you're in an open boat, slop over the bow and force you to take time out from paddling to bail. The point is never to stop or slow down.

If you're a wilderness paddler traveling in a remote setting and with a heavily loaded boat, the measure of your skill is usually just the opposite: how slowly can you make your boat go as the water gets faster and pushier? Can you always just plain stop if you want to?

The two skills are by no means mutually exclusive. Anyone who has precise control of his or her boat and a keen understanding of moving water can function well in either mode. But there is a fundamental difference of ambience and attitude. The race is a game; referees and timekeepers and rescue teams keep a watchful eye. The conditions—as in a laboratory experiment—are controlled. Everyone paddles the same stretch of river on the same day in the same class boat. The variables are in the paddlers themselves, and it is those variables of strength, endurance, and skill that the even playing field of the racecourse and the single measuring stick of speed are meant to test. The race and the lab experiment may have something important to tell us about life, but they are small, encapsulated worlds cordoned off from the messy complexity of life itself.

A canoe trip may not be real life, either, but it comes a lot closer. (Actually, it's realer than real life, and that's why its

173

addicts are as addicted as they are.) The sun rises, and the
sun sets. You sleep and you wake up. You have to stop to
eat and drink and rest. If the river insists on hurrying along
faster and fiercer than you want to go, you have to know
how to put on the brakes. Where the racer is searching out
the fastest line and digging in, trying to outrun the river, the
wilderness traveler is backpaddling, inching and picking her
way down a sneak route on the inside of the bend, letting
the speed of the river slide away under her without taking
her along with it. The racer accepts a few bumps and
scrapes as part of the game. The wilderness paddler wants
to come through with her canoe, her gear, and herself utterly unscathed. Because her boat is heavier and more sluggish than the racer's empty hull, she needs more time and

space to anticipate and complete maneuvers. She wants to be moving downstream so slowly that she can stop her forward progress altogether and back ferry to either side to pick a clearer route, so slowly that if she should foul up and hit a rock the blow will be no worse than running aground on a cobble beach.

If she can't see far enough ahead to know exactly what she's getting into and to know whether she can handle it or not, a couple of flicks of the paddle take her ashore. She stops; she walks; she looks. She knows that slow and steady is what wins in this nonrace. She knows that the price of not stopping can be inordinately high—injury, the loss of a boat, food, and gear; at worst, death; at best, discomfort and delay—and she never lets impatience or fatigue lure her into frothy, unscouted waters.

Unfamiliar whitewater is a clear enough signal to slow down and, if necessary, stop; but there are other signals, too, some of them much more subtle than a roaring river but just as essential to be attuned to. Winokapau Lake in the Churchill River is a narrow lake about thirty-five miles long, and from Fox Island at its west end to Long Point seven miles short of its east end, there are precious few places to camp, none of which are particularly inviting. Most of the shoreline on Winokapau is granite ledges or boulder fields rising out of the water at about forty-five degrees and climbing a thousand feet at that same angle up onto the Labrador plateau. So the strategy is to camp on Fox Island or just short of it and, in your evening prayers, to ask the gods for a nice tail wind out of the west for the next day. If they're unreceptive to that idea, go for a wind-still day or, at the very least, no more than a little breeze out of the east. Then get on the water in good time the next morning, ride your tail wind down to Long Point, make camp with plenty of daylight to spare, and wonder why everybody says paddling twenty-eight miles on Winokapau is such a big deal. Or, if you're not so lucky, set out into the teeth of a nor'easter, pull your insides out against the wind all day, huddle on drenched rock piles as you eat soggy cheese and crackers, and hit Long Point about midnight.

My last Winokapau transit was somewhere in between those two extremes. We didn't get on the water early, but the morning was seductively sunny and calm, the sweetest kind of Indian summer day one could hope for. And so we were seduced. We took our time. We lay back in the boats and soaked in the sun. We explored the grottos and gar-goyle cliffs on the north shore, sat in our boats and watched the falls the old-timers call Whitefall tumble off its ledge and drop straight down into the lake, then pulled ashore for a lazy lunch with hot soup.

In the afternoon we crossed over to the south shore, which offers at least a few more chances for getting off the lake in an emergency than the north, and by six o'clock we still had about eight miles to go to Long Point. The breeze that had come up in the afternoon was dropping, so we decided to cook supper on the shore, then paddle on to Long Point to make camp and sleep.

By the time we were back on the water, the sky had clouded over. It was pitch-dark, no moon, and the lake was glassy smooth. After some initial blinking back and forth with flashlights to check that all five of our canoes were in touch with each other, we settled into those steady, synchro-nized, nearly effortless strokes that make a canoe feel some-thing like a bird in flight. The paddle blades rise and fall in unison, grip, push through, relax, feather, slice up and forward, take hold again, the bird sustained by air, the boat by water.

We are an eerie, ghostly, and lovely flotilla, present to each other only in the soft sounds of our boats cutting through water, the paddles dipping and lifting, the occasional muffled thunk of a paddle shaft on a gunwale. Sometimes a darker darkness looms up to the left or right. We veer apart, and that darkness is gone. A few boat lengths ahead, a match winks as Joe lights a cigarette, and we are again in total darkness.

No one has said a word for half an hour or more. We have all agreed, without discussion, that this black silence is too dear and precious to break. Each boat both lives and moves in it and carries it like a fragile cargo.

I am oblivious to everything but my own bliss. Fortunately, not everyone's attention is totally absorbed by the enchantment of the moment.

"Could we raft up for a minute?" Jerry's voice says out of the blackness. The boats converge. We hang onto each other's gunwales. We are all accounted for. "A squall's coming up," Jerry says. "We better head for shore."

Now that someone has said it, we all realize he is right. The air is suddenly cool and restless. Winokapau has taken a deep breath and is about to let fly with it.

Do we head for the north or south shore? The lake is about a mile wide here. We surely haven't strayed far enough from the south shore to be anywhere near midpoint. South has to be closer, and we start digging for it. No sooner are we underway than the squall hits us broadside, coming straight out of the west down the lake. It's not bad enough to give us any serious trouble, but bad enough that we want to be off the water before it gets any worse.

In my bow, Horace says, "Turn on your light, Bob."

I flick on my headlamp, and within a few minutes a beach of jumbled black rocks heaves into view. Not the ideal place to land, but plenty ideal for now. Before the waves have built enough to start smashing the boats around on the rock, we have them unloaded and lifted up onto the beach.

A few yards down the beach Garrett finds a place large enough and flat enough to pitch his big pyramid tent. Eight will fit into it, just barely, so Jerry and I stretch a tarp over a couple of canoes for a makeshift shelter, toss our sleeping pads and bags inside, and roll in under the thwarts.

Because Jerry had been alert enough to read what the air on the back of his neck was telling him, we were all safely ashore, together, and getting a decent night's rest in our impromptu camp, not scattered about a windy lake in the pitch-dark, wondering what had become of the other canoes and probably not finding out until daylight.

And only when daylight came could we see how much we owed our night's sleep not only to Jerry's prudence but also to Lady Luck. Fifty yards west and fifty yards east of our camp Winokapau's granite cliffs rose straight up out of the water. They'd have made an impossible landing for a mountain goat. We'd hit the only notch in that stretch of shoreline where it was possible to get a boat ashore.

Having had the sleep at Lady Luck Beach that we had orginally planned for Long Point, you might think we'd have just boomed on by the next morning, remarking, perhaps, on what a pretty place Long Point would have been to camp. The sun was bright in the sky; the breeze was at our backs. It was a perfect day for traveling. If we had put our minds to it, we could have bagged a bunch of miles. We could have reached the end of the lake, put the Devil's Hole and Mouni Rapids behind us, and probably gotten down as far as Shoal River or Bear Island, maybe even Cache River, before we made camp.

But of course we did none of that. We had agreed we would stop at Long Point for a midmorning cup of tea, and once we were there at what has to be one of the most exquisite sites on the Churchill River, one cup of tea became two cups. We took off our boots, wriggled our toes in the hot sand, and lay back with hats over eyes for ten-minute soaks in the sun.

We looked down the lake onto the mountain looming yellow and gold with September's aspen and birch. We looked down the long curve of the sand beach here on the lee side of the point. We looked up at the waterfalls tum-

bling down off the plateau like molten silver, and gradually a consensus emerged, unspoken at first, then expressed in words and happily seized upon by all. This was too beautiful a place to pass through as if it were an airport. This was the kind of place where anyone in his right mind would stop, take some walks alone, watch the sun move across the sky, pay thanks and homage.

So we stayed. Teatime blended into lunchtime. We broke out the pea soup, the peanut butter and cheese and pepperoni, some German chocolate bars that Fred, commander of the German air force contingent at Goose Bay, had brought along in his large, deep pack full of German goodies. We unloaded the canoes, rolled them over on shore, stowed paddles, poles, and life jackets under them.

Because this is late September in Labrador, we are prepared for the snow, cold rain, and wind that come with the leading edge of winter. We carry three roomy cotton tents equipped with sheet-steel stoves. No matter what the weather does, we can cook, eat, and relax in snug comfort.

Today, though, we are basking in the elements, not seeking shelter from them. Here on the beach, in the lee of the point, we are almost untouched by the wind that is raising whitecaps out on the lake. With our tents set up on the edge of the woods and our firewood already cut, we settle into those social and solitary pleasures of a layover day.

Garrett goes off to see if there's some relatively painless route up to the waterfall on the hill behind the point. I dig clean socks and underwear out of my duffel and wander up the beach. A swim in Labrador in late September may sound like madness, but on this day it is not. "Swim," of course, is a misnomer. The sun may be warm, but the water remains forbiddingly, lethally cold, as it does year round.

You dive in, come up bellowing, take perhaps a few flopping strokes, and clamber out. In the time it takes me to rinse out a sweaty T-shirt and socks, standing shin deep in the water, my feet turn blue, and my bones begin to ache. But it is refreshing, bracing, cleansing, downright purifying; and emboldened by one fool's example, others emulate it. Carolyn and Cheryl dive in, come up shrieking, towel off, and stretch out on the warm sand.

It's midafternoon now. Most of us have been in the water for a quick splash and are luxuriating in clean clothes. Our boots, which have had no relief from our sweaty feet for the last few days, are basking in the sun, and as it moves across the sky, we turn the boot tops toward it, like flowers, so they can suck as much of that warmth as possible down into their dank depths. Sleeping bags festoon the alders, and when we crawl into those bags tonight, the smell of the sun will still be in them. Socks, underwear, raingear, anything that anyone feels needs an airing is hung on the brush or the drikhi, and from a distance our camp looks like a half-acre Christmas tree.

Horace is the last to go for his swim. He emerges from the woods in blue Fruit of the Loom skivvies. A born Labradorian who first came up this river at the age of twelve to trap with his father, Horace has spent most of his life in the Labrador bush. Now, at sixty-eight, he is still very much in traveling trim. As he heads for the water, his towel over his shoulder, he grins at us loungers and says, "Photos anyone?"

It is our great pleasure and privilege to be traveling this river with Horace. Not only does he know its every riffle and current, cove and island, he also knows its human history as only a player in that history could. There are a few older men still left in Goose Bay, men in their eighties now, who were part of the old trapping culture and who were in their mature years when Horace first traveled with them as a boy. They, too, know where to find all the old trappers' cabins—or tilts, as they are called here—along the river; but Horace is probably the only man still traveling the river whose lifetime and experience reach back before the U.S. Air Force came to Goose Bay and long before the engineers got their greasy little fingers on Churchill Falls and transformed central Labrador into a sluiceway for hydropower.

Whenever Horace pulls ashore and disappears into a jungle of alders seemingly never penetrated before by humankind, we all follow him eagerly to what is always another historic site. Back up on the higher ground, above the highwater line, he leads us to a caved-in tilt. The roof has gone down long since, and its remnants are moss-covered now, but—to my eye at any rate—these ruins have a dignity about them and waken a sense of reverence and respect to rival, if not exceed, anything that the monuments of Greece and Rome have ever inspired in me.

The craftsmanship accounts for some of that. The long, clean cuts in the notches of the logs bespeak a razor-sharp axe in the hands of a man who knew how to use it. The door is broken in half, but its joints, all made without nails or glue, are still snug and tight. The old tins that once held Klim dried milk or butter or bacon would be trash anywhere else, but here they are a reminder that men used to paddle, pole, and track canoes loaded with their winter supplies *up* this river, some as far as two hundred miles. And then they would portage one thousand feet up onto the Height of Land and travel still farther into the interior before setting up their fur paths.

So these abandoned tilts and the axe heads, traps, and tins rusting in their remains are monuments to physical strength and endurance, canoemanship, woodcraft, and hunting and trapping skills that make even reasonably accomplished amateur outdoor folk look like tenderfoot Scouts. They are also monuments to an intact society peopled by men who, though scattered across three hundred miles of wild country, would drop in on their "neighbors" in adjoining trapping territories fifteen or twenty miles up- or downstream and would pass mail and packages of cookies and fudge on to their ultimate destination many miles farther on upriver.

Here at Long Point, Horace has seen as many as thirty tents where we are camped now. This is just the time of year when the trappers were heading upriver, and Long Point was the natural place to camp before paddling the length of Winokapau the next day. So we are stopping here not just because this is a lovely place, which it surely is, but also because it is an historic place, peopled with spirits Horace knows well and whose acquaintance we feel honored to make.

The river keeps rushing on to the sea. We let it rush. It has its reasons. We have ours for slowing down, for stopping for a few minutes, for a few hours, maybe even for a whole day. Half the art of paddling, maybe more than half, is knowing how and when to stop.

$\mathcal{W}$ATERFALL CHORUS

I SOMETIMES HEAR singing in waterfalls—not always, but given the right kind of falls and the right conditions. I don't ever remember hearing it in a big, high-volume falls, for instance, and I don't remember hearing it in broad daylight either. Maybe it was there; and, preoccupied with daytime preoccupations or deafened to underlying tones by the surface roar, I just didn't hear what was in fact there. I don't know. But I do know that at one of my very favorite places to camp in all of Maine (if not the world) I hear this waterfall music quite often. The site is on the shore of a lake, and about a hundred yards back from the shore the outlet brook from a trout pond half a mile back up in the hills makes a final drop of eight or ten feet before flowing on out past the campsite and into the lake.

The falls are small enough and far enough away that they do not overwhelm your senses, pummeling at your ears and brain and forcing you to raise your voice to be heard over them; but they are always there, a companionable, unobtrusive presence if you are not specifically attending to them and much more if you are.

I find I'm most attentive just after I've crawled into my sleeping bag and have nothing to do but bask in the sweet torpor that follows a day of paddling or climbing around among the hills and backcountry ponds surrounding this chain of pure, pellucid lakes. As I lie there in the darkness, what I hear first is just the rush of the water. But then, above or behind the sound of the falls, the voices gradually chime in. They are like nothing else I've ever heard, but if I had to find a comparison, the closest I could come would

be a cross between gospel singing and plainsong. The voices don't have the punch and drama of gospel singers. They are lighter; their range is narrower; but they soar, fade out, come in again. Sometimes there is only one voice; sometimes many blending in a harmonic, ringing chant. There are no words, of course, nor are there any very low or very high registers, any hotshot basses or sopranos.

To call these voices angelic conveys something of their quality, but it is all wrong in the sense that they are not otherworldly. On the contrary, worldly is exactly what they are—the voices of this world made audible in or through the water, and to identify them with any of our little deities or demigods or woodsy Walt Disney spirits is to violate them and cheapen them. Sigurd Olson wrote of the singing wilderness. It does sing. We needn't say more.

$\mathcal{W}$ET FEET

YOU MAY BE able to stave them off for a while. You may be able to pussyfoot around and keep your toes out of the drink if you're paddling on lakes or easy rivers where you never have to wade or line or portage and where every landing you make is on such gentle, sloping shores that your hardly get the soles of your boots damp. But if you're out for a day of whitewater, you'll probably soak your head as well as your feet; and if you make extended trips into territory where unrunnable rapids and bog wallowing are the order of the day, you can count on wetting your feet again and again and again, often up to your armpits.

You're going to get wet, so you might as well just get wet and stay wet. That sounds like a simple strategy, but it is open to a number of interpretations and refinements.

The first school of thought is the Permanent L. L. Bean Boot school. Bean's leather-top rubbers are wonderful canoeing boots. They're light and flexible. The rubber foot is waterproof, and with enough layers of Sno-Seal lathered onto them to make them glow in the dark, the tops are as close to waterproof as leather can get. On trips that don't make you wade much above your ankles, you may even make it from start to finish with dry feet, barring accidents

187

and miscalculations. At the start of a Machias River trip a couple of years ago, I slid my canoe into the water at Fifth Machias Lake on a breezy May afternoon, then turned around to pick up a pack and begin loading the boat. In those few seconds, the wind sent the empty boat sailing out onto the pond, and I had to run into the water up to my middle to catch it. I might as well have poured a pailful of water into each boot before I put them on and been done with it.

But on the right kind of trip and barring the aforementioned accidents and miscalculations, Bean boots may keep your feet dry, from the outside, that is. If you're given to perspiration and athlete's foot, two weeks of warm weather will have your toes breeding fungus like a well-manured mushroom farm.

On a wading and wallowing kind of trip, the moment of truth will come sooner or later. The Permanent L. L. Bean Boot Wearer (PLLBBW) is making his way down a small stream that suddenly ceases to be a stream and scatters all over the landscape in a huge beaver flowage. The water slithers through alder brakes, crawls under tangled blowdowns, slides glassily over ancient tree trunks. Just scouting out a route here, not to mention horsing a boat through, calls for knee-deep, possibly hip-deep slogging. The PLLBBW is standing in the stern of his boat. He hesitates for just a moment, during which you can practically read on his forehead what is going through his mind. "Do I really want to do this? Do I really want to live in wet boots for the next twelve days? Oh, well...." And in he goes. And for the next twelve days he gives no more thought to wading in and out of the water than your average moose would; he climbs in and out of his dank boots and socks without a peep of complaint. PLLBBWs are stoic sorts who have better things to do with their time than fret about minor discomforts and can't be bothered cluttering up their packs with extra footwear.

The second wet-foot school is the Sneaker, Sock, and Neoprene Bootie school (SSNB). If the weather and water are relatively warm, you wear the socks—wool or polyester pile. Wool is more comfortable but loses its shape and wears out quickly with constant wetting. The artificial fiber socks dry quicker, keep their shape better, and last longer. For those days when you're in and out of the water repeatedly all day and the water is just a few degrees short of ice, the neoprene booties are a godsend. After twelve hours in them, your feet may look like fish that have gone belly up, and I don't know how many days running you could wear them before your toenails would fall out and your skin start peeling off. But they do keep you warm. The performance of sneakers or running shoes can be much improved by gluing old felt insoles on the bottoms of them with contact cement. The felt not only gives you a little extra protection but also vastly improves traction on slippery rocks.

Those who prefer the sneaker-sock combination usually have something of a dramatic flair. Pulling on damp socks at 6:00 A.M. when there is frost on the ground can inspire some impressive histrionics. I remember fondly our traveling companion Kimberly, who brightened many a Labrador morning with her lamentations: "EEEEKKK! O God! Oh, no! I can't stand it. Aarrgggh! Help, oh, help, please, no! Aaaahhh! Sweet heaven, how can you do this to me? I'm innocent! I swear it! Spare me! What have I done to deserve this?"

And that was just for the right foot.

189

The third school, to which I belong, is the Comfort Above Convenience school (CAC). A CAC tries to stay dry as much as possible but will bow to the inevitble when the inevitable is truly inevitable. I start out in the Bean boots and have the sneakers, socks, and booties handy in my day pack. When the time for wading comes, I change into the sneakers and stay in them for as long as it looks like the wading is likely to last: another hour, the rest of the day, the next two days. But in the evening, I've always got the dry Bean boots to change back into; and whenever the hauling and wallowing are over for the foreseeable future, I can dig out the Bean boots again and tie the sneakers out on the deck to dry in the sun. It sounds like a foolproof system, right? The best of both worlds. But just wait. The river will get you yet.

You've made camp for the night, changed into your dry boots, and wandered upstream a ways with your fly rod.

190

You've been fishing for an hour or so, caught and released a couple of respectable trout, but the one that is a bit more than respectable has eluded you. The riverbank is fairly open, and with a little rock hopping you've been able to get yourself into strategic locations where you can roll out a long back cast, cover quite a lot of water, and still keep your feet dry. But now you see a beautiful midstream eddy where you know the very fish you're after is lurking. You can't reach it from where you are. Even if your cast is flawless and you lay out as much line as you and your rod are capable of handling, your fly will still fall six or seven feet short of where you want it.

But about six or seven feet out from the rock you're standing on now is another rock, the perfect vantage point for casting into that eddy. To get there, you will have to wade up to your knees. Walking back down to camp to change back into your wet sneakers is too much of a nuisance. And besides, this is the witching hour. You know that if you don't make your bid for that fish within the next ten minutes, the magic moment will be gone for tonight.

"Come, come now," the more prosaic half of your head says. "What do you know about witching hours and magic moments? What makes you so sure that fish is there? And it may not be the least bit interested in your fly. Do you really want to soak your boots in pursuit of a fish that may not exist? Or that may be so replete that it's burping and belching down there, nauseated at the very thought of another mouthful?"

Torn between caution and passion, you hesitate, then toss caution to the breeze. You're up that rock now, your boots full of water, your line rolling out into the twilight, your mouth nearly adrool with frantic anticipation. You

191

cast, you twitch your bucktail past that fish's nose. You cast again. You work every inch of that eddy. Nothing. You can't believe it, but then again you can. How much of your life, after all, have you spent in pursuit of phantom fish? Isn't it the rule rather than the exception that you find yourself standing wet-footed and empty-handed on a dark riverbank?

And so, grinning happily, you take another cast and another and another. Then you wade back to shore, sit on a rock, tip each leg up high enough to drain most of the water out of your boots, and head back to camp.

"Squish, squish," your feet say, living proof that in the hands of a perfect fool even foolproof systems fail.

$\mathcal{W}$ILDERNESS

ABOUT THE BEST reason I can think of for owning and paddling a canoe is that it can take me into wilderness. And what, you may ask, is so great about wilderness? The silence, for one thing. In real wilderness, silence is not just quiet, which is the absence of noise. It is the voice of the living earth, unmuddied by aural clutter.

I live in the country, which is much quieter than the city, but even in the country there is a lot of noise: the cars of people commuting to work, the machines that build the houses, cut down the trees, haul the gravel, paint the stripes down the middle of the roads, fly around in the sky, split quiet lakes in half, whine across the top of the snow.

In the country, you experience blessed periods of quiet, and quiet is surely a great treasure. But in the wilderness you are surrounded by the voices of silence, and they are a greater treasure still.

What else is wilderness? The water you can drink; the air you can see through; Mars climbing up over the horizon, splitting into a mirage of double Mars, and dancing a little jig with itself. Wilderness is a ghostly rainbow arching white across the night sky under a full moon.

There are lots of highfalutin texts about wilderness experi-

193

ence—visions, epiphanies, all manner of mystical stuff. Davidson and Rugge, who have spent enough time in the bush to know what they're talking about, have this to say about wilderness being "a quality of the heart, something *inside* [us]. Nonsense. The wilderness is plain open space, the sheer physical presence of the earth unwinding without us people."

That sheer physical presence can affect our inner state, but I think what is going on is pretty simple and straightforward. The "wilderness high" is no more nor less than the delight we take in all that plain open space, in a world absolutely free of our own clutter, a world that has not suffered the slightest infringement of man the tool-making, dam-building, road-building, mine-digging, tree-cutting, water-polluting animal. Just to see it all as it was in the beginning, that in itself is such a delight and a privilege that we get "high," which is simply to say that we are happier than we can ever be in the normal course of our lives.

The enjoyment of wilderness, it seems to me, is a privilege we should have to earn, not a right we can claim. And if we are going to have any wilderness left in this world, we'll have to establish a principle of earned access to it. That means we'll have to set aside large territories where aircraft are illegal. It means that if you want to get into real back-country, you'll have to work to get there. You can't buy you're way in. You can't substitute the power of petroleum and money for the truly earned power of knowing how to handle your boat on the river, to keep yourself warm and dry, to feed yourself, and take care of your companions as they take care of you. We'll have to make it illegal for mere wealth to buy its way into our remaining wilderness.

If you object that these are elitist ideas, let me try to con-

vince you otherwise. Since when has travel by foot or by paddle been elitist? These are the most primitive modes of transportation known to humankind. Anyone who walks or paddles is reverting to the primitive. The elitists are the people in the airplanes, in the four-wheel-drive trucks, on the snowmobiles and ATVs.

And what about the old and infirm? I think I'm old enough to address that question with some kind of realism. What will I do for wilderness if or when I'm too decrepit to walk or paddle into it? I'll do without. I'll regret it, but I hope I'll do my regretting with good grace, not bitterness. Because that is simply the natural course of things. When I am past the time when I have the physical strength to get where I'd like to go, then I'll yield that privilege to those who do. I won't ask that a road be built for me or a plane be hired for me, so that I can violate wild places out of my personal yen for them. They will get on without me. I am as grass. Grass withers, the flower fades; but may the word that is wilderness stand forever.

NOTES ON READINGS AND GEAR

READINGS

Of the many how-to books on canoeing and canoe camping, there are five I find particularly useful.

Most how-to books on canoeing make passing mention of the essential wilderness skills of poling, lining, and portaging, but the only book to treat them in a detailed and authoritative manner is Garrett Conover's *Beyond the Paddle* (Tilbury House, 1991). Conover also introduces the reader to the use of ice hooks and sleds for late fall and early spring travel.

James West Davidson and John Rugge's *The Complete Wilderness Paddler* (Alfred J. Knopf, 1975; Vintage paperback edition, 1983) lives up to its name and does so with great verve, style, and humor. Davidson and Rugge (admirers of Huck Finn) hang their how-to information on the narrative of a Moisie River trip. The yarn of the journey, plus Davidson and Rugge's considerable talents as writers, make this one of the world's most readable and enjoyable how-to books.

At one point in his *Canoeing Wild Rivers* (ICS Books, revised, expanded edition, 1989), Cliff Jacobson asks his friend Bob Dannert to define the word "expert," and Dannert replies, "Details." Jacobson himself is the detail man par excellence, and when he goes into details of packing, canoe rigging, campcraft—you name it—he dots all his i's and crosses all his t's. Appendixes contain lists of sources for information and equipment.

Bill Mason's *Path of the Paddle: An Illustrated Guide to the Art of Canoeing* (Key Porter Books, 1984) is an excellent book on paddling technique and whitewater paddling from the wilderness canoeist's perspective. The many step-by-step photographs and diagrams make this book particularly helpful. And its companion volume, *Song of the Paddle: An Illustrated Guide to Wilderness Camping* (published in Canada by Key Porter Books and in the USA by NorthWord Press Inc., 1988), covers canoe camping with the same thoroughness and visual accessibility.

GEAR

BAGS, BOXES, BASKETS

The classic Duluth pack is made by Duluth Tent and Awning, Inc., 1610 West Superior Street, Box 6024, Duluth, MN 55806. Consult Cliff Jacobson's *Canoeing Wild Rivers* for details on the waterproofing and efficient use of Duluth packs. The Superior Pack Co., CLG Enterprises, P.O. Box 6687, Minneapolis, MN 55406, lives up to its name, making a superior Duluth pack.

A number of companies—among them, L. L. Bean, Inc., Freeport, ME 04033; North American Pack Basket Co., P.O. Box 47, Kempton, PA 19529; and Piragis Northwoods Company, 105 N. Central Avenue, Ely, MN 55731—carry packbaskets. Stephen Zeh, Basketmaker, P.O. Box 381, Temple, ME 04984, makes superb—but extremely expensive—packbaskets. Try your local army-surplus store for rubberized GI laundry bags.

For Northwest River bags the place to go is Northwest River Supplies, P.O. Box 9186, Moscow, ID 83843. The 2.2-cubic-foot size is just right for one person's clothes, sleeping bag, and sleeping pad.

BUOYANCY

Extrasport, 5305 N. W. 35 Court, Miami, FL 33142, makes life jackets much favored by whitewater paddlers. They can be ordered directly from Extrasport, also from Wildwater Designs, 230 Penllyn Pike, Penllyn, PA 19422 and Northwest River Supplies (see address above). Other popular brands are Harishok, Omega, Seda, and Stearns.

COMFORT

Therm-a-Rest mattresses are available from outfitters and sporting-goods stores everywhere.

Snow and Nealley, Box 876, Bangor, ME 04401, does not retail directly, but its axes and other logging tools are sold in many hardware stores. Mail-order sources are the Seneca Falls Saw Co., P.O. Box 7875, Seneca Falls, NY 13148, and Lehman Hardware and Appliances, P. O. Box 41, Kidron, OH 44636.

EFFICIENCY APARTMENT

Consult Cliff Jacobson's chapter "Canoe Tents Are Different" in *Canoeing Wild Rivers* for a good summary of desirable qualities in a nylon, three-season tent. On a canoe trip, you can afford the luxury of carrying a four-person tent for every two people. The Eureka Timberline is one model that has served canoeists well.

Nylon (and sometimes polyethylene) tarps are standard fare in most outfitting stores including L. L. Bean (see address above) and Campmor, P.O. Box 997, Paramus, NJ 07653-0997. A source for cotton tarps and wall tents is Tentsmiths, Box 496, North Conway, NH 03860. A cotton tarp or tent, properly cared for, can last many years and justify the extra initial expense. The trick is finding a fabric that is light enough (4 to 7 oz.) to carry easily and has a high enough thread count (minimum 220) to be waterproof. With light cotton fabrics, supplementary treatment with a product such as Camp Dry (made by Kiwi Brands, Inc., Douglassville, PA 19518) is sometimes needed to keep them waterproof. Campmor carries a 7-oz., 160-count cotton poplin, treated with a water repellent and a fire retardant, as yard goods. I have no experience with it.

Sheet-steel stoves can be found in Canadian outfitting stores. Bill Mason lists some sources in *Song of the Paddle* and also provides plans for building your own stove.

FLEECE AND WOOL

Johnson, Pendleton, and Woolrich are familiar names in most stores where woolen outdoor clothing is sold. The C. C. Filson Company, 1246 First Avenue South, Seattle, WA 98134 (catalog available at that address) makes the ultimate in heavy-duty wool clothing.

NORTH WOODS STROKE

Photocopies of Garrett Conover's article "Traveling with Ease and Grace: A Traditional Northwoods Stroke" in *The Entry-Level Guide to Canoeing and Kayaking* (vol. 2, 1984) can be purchased from *Canoe* magazine, P.O. Box 3146, Kirkland, WA 98083.

For another look at the north woods stroke, see Lynn Franklin, "Paddling like an Ancient" (*WoodenBoat*, No. 55, Nov/Dec 1983), available from The WoodenBoat Catalog, P.O. Box 78, Brooklin, ME 04616.

PADDLES

For detailed instructions (including plans) on making a north woods paddle, see Rick Waters, "The North Woods Paddle" (*WoodenBoat*, No. 67, Nov/Dec 1985), available from The WoodenBoat Catalog. North Woods Ways, P. O. Box 286, Dover-Foxcroft, ME 04426, sells full-scale blueprints for 5- and 6-foot north woods paddles (both on the same sheet) plus a reprint of the Waters article.

Mohawk paddles are for sale just about everywhere. The maufacturer's address is 963 North Highway 427, Longwood, FL 32750.

PEANUT BUTTER

The mailing address for Walnut Acres is Penns Creek, PA 17862.

POLING

Most canoe poles are homemade. The simplest route is to find a dead but still sound black spruce no thicker than one-and-three-quarter inches at what will be the lower end of your pole. Cut the pole eleven or twelve feet long; slice the branches off as close to the trunk as you can; peel the pole; smooth the knots and any other irregularities with a drawknife or spokeshave. The point isn't to create a perfectly round, straight pole by paring away all the natural curves in the tree but to get rid of any nicks or bumps that will irritate the hands. Sand for a final smoothing, and put on a couple of coats of boiled linseed oil.

The great disadvantage of the natural pole is its imbalance—thicker and heavier at the butt, skinnier and lighter at the tip. Traditional polers use only one end of the pole, but I confess I've been corrupted enough by racing style that I at least like to have the option of using either end of the pole; and for that, you need a pole of uniform thickness for its entire length. Also, even if you never use both ends, a perfectly smooth, balanced pole is easier to use. You can find instructions for making this kind of pole of ash or spruce in Jerry Stelmok's *Building the Maine Guide Canoe* (International Marine Publishing Co., 1980). Out of print at the moment, this book will be reissued by Lyons and Burford, Publishers, 31 West Twenty-first Street, New York, NY 10010, in spring 1992. Garrett Conover's *Beyond the Paddle* also has instructions for making poles.

L. L. Bean still sells a twelve-foot ash pole equipped with an iron shoe at its Freeport store, but this is not a catalog item. Aluminum poles are made of drawn aluminum tubing, 6061-T6, 1.125-inch outside diameter, .058-inch wall thickness, which you can buy at aluminum-supply houses. The ends have to be plugged with watertight plugs of wood or plastic so that the pole will float if dropped in the water. One way to get a ready-made aluminum pole is to write to the Poling Committee, American Canoe Association, P.O. Box 1190, Newington, VA 22122, and find out where the next poling event near you is. ACA polers have developed a hand-to-hand distribution system. Also, the poling committee will be happy to provide detailed instructions for making your own. A commercial source is Mad River Canoe, P.O. Box 207, Waitsfield, VT 05673.

REAL FOOD

A concise and helpful book on trail nutrition and menus is Dorcas Miller's *The Healthy Trail Food Book* (revised edition, The East Woods Press, 1980), unfortunately no longer in print.

RIVER PIGS, TIN CANS, AND OTHER CRAFT

Canoe magazine's annual buyer's guide, published each year in the December issue, always provides a quick rundown on the basics of canoe design along with its listing of canoe makers and the various models they offer.

Anyone interested in the wood-and-canvas canoe will find membership in the Wooden Canoe Heritage Association, Ltd., P.O. Box 226, Blue Mountain Lake, NY 12812, informative and fun.

Some leading makers of wood-and-canvas canoes in North America are:

Alex Comb
Stewart River Boatworks
Route 1, Box 203 B
Two Harbors, MN 55616

Don Fraser
176 Woodstock Road
Fredricton, N.B. E3B 2H5

Steve Kilbridge
Temagami Canoe Co.
Box 20
Temagami, Ontario P0H 2H0

Jim Leavitt
Leavitt Quality Craft
RFD 1, Box 1549
Hampden, ME 04444

Tom MacKenzie
The Loon Works
525 Orchard Drive
Madison, WI 53711

Jack McGreivey
McGreivey's Canoe Shop
Route 2, Box 139
Cato, NY 13033

Bill Miller
Miller Canoes
RR 1, Plaster Rock
Nictau, N.B. E0J 1W0

Scott Mills
Raven Boats
9 North Yukon Drive
Ely, MN 55731

Joe Seliga
Seliga Canoes
244 East Pattison Street
Ely, MN 55731

Jerry Stelmok
Island Falls Canoe
RFD 3, Box 76
Dover-Foxcroft, ME 04426

Horace Strong
Strong's Canoe Yard
Craftsbury Common, VT 05827

Rollin Thurlow
Northwoods Canoe Co.
RFD 3, Box 118-A2
Dover-Foxcroft, ME 04426

WET FEET

L. L. Bean boots are available from—of course—L. L. Bean, Inc.

Neoprene wet-suit booties come in different configurations. The ones usually called "wetsocks" are just that: socks meant to be worn inside sneakers. I prefer these because you can then wear your sneakers with regular socks as well. More substantial are "wetshoes," which are neoprene booties bonded to soles of varying thicknesses, very few of which are designed for heavy-duty wilderness-river wading. The Alpina Wet Shoe incorporates a neoprene bootie into a more substantial-looking shoe, but then you don't have the versatility that separate wetsocks and sneakers give you.

All the outfitters specializing in paddling gear (Northwest River Supply, Wildwater Designs, etc.) and many general outdoor outfitters (L. L. Bean, REI, etc.) carry wetsocks and wetshoes.

A *Canoeist's Sketchbook* was
designed and typeset in Goudy Old Style by
Kate Mueller/Chelsea Green Publishing Company.
It was printed on Glatfelter, an acid-free paper,
by Capital City Press.